Math without Fear

D1711531

Related Titles of Interest

Math without Fear

A Guide for Preventing Math Anxiety in Children

Joseph G. R. Martinez
with
Nancy C. Martinez

Allyn and Bacon
Boston • London • Toronto • Sydney • Tokyo • Singapore

Library of Congress Cataloging-in-Publication Data

Martinez, Joseph G. R.
    Math without fear : a guide for preventing math anxiety in
children / by Joseph G. R. Martinez with Nancy C. Martinez.
        p.   cm.
    Includes bibliographical references and index.
    ISBN 0-205-16021-2
    1. Math anxiety.   2. Mathematics—Study and teaching.
I. Martinez, Nancy C. (Nancy Conrad)   II. Title.
QA11.M318   1996
372.7—dc20   95-42262
                                                          CIP

Printed in the United States of America

10   9   8   7   6   5   4   3   2   1   00   99   98   97   96

*To Sister Laetitia and Sister Francis,
my first and best math teachers, and to
my students who overcame math anxiety to
become fearless mathematicians*

Contents

Preface

This is a book for elementary classroom teachers—the front-line, in-the-trenches superheroes of education who must teach mathematics whether they like it or not.

Rather than a concept-by-concept guide to teaching the standard or an innovative math curriculum, the book presents a philosophy and a pedagogy for math teaching that integrate the affective and the cognitive domains of learning and focus on the issue that affects both teachers and students: math anxiety. Drawing techniques from educational psychology, I place math studies within the larger contexts of learning and cognition, develop therapies, and set guidelines.

From the teacher's perspective, the book takes a metacognitive view of math learning. I encourage teachers to assess personal math histories, skills, and attitudes—that is, to observe and think about their own math learning behaviors—and then to use these self-assessments to gain insights about children's attitudes and behaviors. From the children's perspective, the book emphasizes active, hands-on learning, pedagogies to match cognitive development, and systems and strategies that empower them to share the responsibility for their own learning.

My purposes in writing the book were, first, to present a guide for preventing math anxiety in children and, second, to develop techniques for making children confident, fearless mathematicians. Some of the basic premises underlying my work include the following:

1. That the best cure for math anxiety is prevention
2. That the best antidote to math anxiety is math confidence
3. That every child can learn math successfully
4. That every teacher can teach math successfully
5. That math studies should be based on active and interactive experiences
6. That math studies should be diverse and flexible
7. That math curricula should be challenging but matched to children's cognitive development

8. That teachers need a repertoire of math pedagogies to fit children's development, the demands of the curriculum, and the learning contexts
9. That learning systems and technology should empower students to achieve and
   to learn more instead of restricting or limiting learning
10. That gender, race, or ethnic background do not handicap children's math learn-
    ing and that math is a multicultural, equal-opportunity subject.

How the book is used depends on the individual teacher's needs and interests.
Key topics, such as gender and empowerment issues, are listed in the index or the
table of contents. Individual chapters offer assessment tools for diagnosing teachers' or students' math anxieties and strategies for coping with those anxieties. Other
chapters present rationales and examples for making math-learning enjoyable and
for teaching math with games and activities. Throughout the book, numerous illustrations on figures and charts provide a visual dimension to the theories and methods discussed. There are tests for assessing attitudes, skills, and behaviors; guidelines for developing lesson plans; and checklists for assessing various aspects of
math learning or math teaching. At the end of each chapter are questions to think
about or to discuss with other teachers; activities that apply chapter concepts; and
a short annotated list of readings for those who want or need to explore further some
specific theory, concept, method, or idea covered in that specific chapter.

Acknowledgments

I would like to express my appreciation to the many people who have helped with the writing of *Math without Fear*. My students, past and present, have provided much of the material, both by their experiences as math learners and as a testing ground for the techniques, activities, and assessment tools described throughout the book. My teaching colleagues at several different schools have been the subject of numerous anecdotes—a liberty for which I beg pardon if the stories seem negative and express my thanks if they are positive. Both Carolyn Cadney and Christine Fernsler offered valuable criticism and advice in their reviews of the manuscript. I would also like to thank Mylan Jaixen whose initial interest in and enthusiasm for the project spearheaded the effort; Nancy Forsyth, whose insights and guidance have made this a better book and whose encouragement has spurred its completion; Kate Wagstaffe, who saw us through the trials and tribulations of production; and Rebecca Shannon, the typesetter who sent a word of encouragement when we needed it most. I very much appreciate my family's understanding of the long evenings and weekends spent working at the computer. I love all of you and I promise to throw out the trash and clean litter boxes as soon as possible. Last but not least, I would love to thank Nancy, my wife, who co-wrote this book with me. After twenty-plus years of discussing the relationships between learning math and reading and writing, we should have something to say.

J. G. R. M.

Math without Fear

1

The Multiple Faces of Mathematics Anxiety

"Math anxiety," a teacher told me recently, "is a figment of the imagination—a poor student's excuse for failure."

"It's an inevitable response to a difficult subject," explained another, more sympathetic but equally unconcerned teacher. "Ignore it and it will go away."

"Math anxiety is a stop sign," said a third teacher. "It means stop the math lesson and move on to something more pleasant."

"Math anxiety is caused by forcing left-brain students to study a right-brain subject," asserted a fourth. "It's the natural outcome of an unnatural curriculum requirement. Not everyone can learn math."

While the comments are as diverse as the commentators, none satisfactorily answers the question: *What is math anxiety?* Is it a feeling, an attitude, an emotional condition? Is it a learning deficiency, a response to a learning deficiency, or the cause of a learning deficiency? Is it a neurosis to be treated by mental health professionals or an easily remediated response to gaps in knowledge? Is it acquired like a communicable disease or inherited like a genetic defect? Can it be cured? Can it be prevented? Can it be diagnosed and measured and understood sufficiently to develop regimens for treatment or intervention?

The answers to these questions are neither simple nor universal. One person's math anxiety could be knowledge-based—the result of inadequate instruction in basic operations; another's could be tied to shaming behaviors, such as being sent to the chalkboard to work arithmetic problems. One person may have learned math anxiety from a math-anxious teacher, another from a math-anxious parent. For some, anxiety may be linked to all numbers; for others, only to some operations.

Moreover, whatever its origins, the course of math anxiety rarely runs smoothly; it follows a tortuous path, picking up additional baggage along the way. A person who does not understand numbers will soon learn to fear them, and a person who fears numbers will not easily understand them. Avoiding math in the form of homework or study assignments generates additional negative experiences such as failing grades, missed recesses or "Carlos/Carlotta-can't-add" notes to parents. And negative experiences lead to further avoidance in a cycle as difficult to stop as it is easy to begin.

Math Anxiety as a Construct

To understand math anxiety, we must first recognize its complexity. Math anxiety is not a discrete condition, and a case of math anxiety rarely, if ever, follows a straightforward, single-cause/single-effect, linear progression. Instead, math anxiety is a construct. It has multiple causes and multiple effects, interacting in a tangle that defies simple diagnosis and simplistic remedies.

Figure 1-1 shows some of the factors involved in the math problem-solving process. If positive elements from the affective and/or the cognitive domains dominate the problem-solving process, math learning will include confidence as a by-product. If negative elements dominate, the by-product will be anxiety.

In either case, the problem-solving process proceeds in a context that encompasses feelings about math from the affective domain and knowledge about math from the cognitive domain. When Miss Wormwood sends Calvin to the chalkboard,

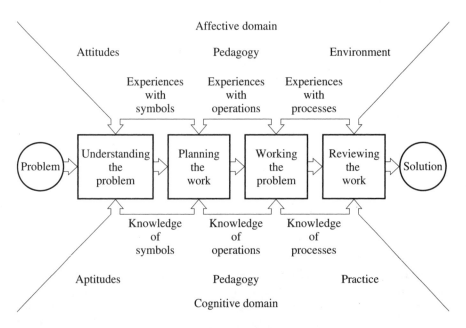

FIGURE 1-1   The Process of Solving Math Problems

she has dual affective and cognitive purposes: to punish Calvin for not paying attention and to teach him to subtract. Calvin sidesteps the lesson by not even trying to work the problem and avoids the punishment by scoring an imaginary victory over his teacher. The result is negative all around. Calvin has not learned to subtract, and the structure he has been building of resistance to math learning has been strengthened.

When Calvin claims to be a "math atheist," he is showing us that his math anxiety has grown to the point that it blocks out learning. More often, however, math anxiety simply interferes with learning by slowing down or distorting the process. In Figure 1-2, a typical math-anxiety construct overshadows working an addition problem that mixes single- and double-digit numbers.

To understand the problem and devise a plan to solve it, the student must draw on previous learning about numbers, math symbols, and addition; however, confusion about carrying numbers and about the relationship between numbers and real things interferes. To work the problem and review the work for accuracy, the student should be able to draw on past practice that has developed a feeling for numbers, but neglecting math lessons and homework has limited this student's facility with manipulating numbers. Throughout the problem-solving process, memories and feelings from past math-learning experiences generate a background of mental noise, like static on a poorly tuned radio: "You failed before. You'll be in trouble if you fail again. Mom will be mad. The kids will laugh at you. The teacher will give you an F. He'll write a note to your mom. You're hopeless. You can't do this. You're math dumb." With so much interference in the problem-solving process, the student's chances of finding the solution are diminished while the chances for being confident about any solution are almost nil.

Notice that the math-anxiety construct is not exclusively a product of the affective domain. The cognitive domain contributes as well. Moreover, the interaction of cognitive and affective elements produces the tangle that defies simple solutions.

Math Anxiety and the Cognitive Domain

The cognitive domain of learning might best be described as its logical component. Logical thought processes, information storage and retrieval, aptitude for learning math, match of learning readiness and teaching strategies—all belong to the cognitive domain. This domain affects math anxiety when there are gaps in knowledge,

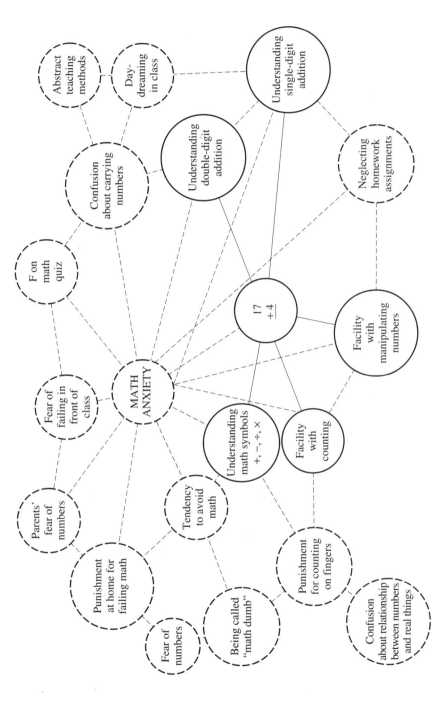

FIGURE 1-2   A Math-Anxiety Construct

when information is mislearned, and when learning readiness and teaching strategies are mismatched.

1. *Gaps in knowledge:* "It all goes back to grade school," a math-anxious student teacher told me. "I never learned my times tables." Not learning the times tables probably means that the student never understood the relationship between addition and multiplication—that 6×6 is really just shorthand for $6 + 6 + 6 + 6 + 6 + 6$ or that 3×10, $3 + 3 + 3 + 3 + 3 + 3 + 3 + 3 + 3 + 3$, 10×3, and $10 + 10 + 10$ are different versions of the same problem. This gap in turn makes it difficult for the student to understand $6\overline{)36}$, $\frac{36}{6}$, and $\frac{1}{6} \times \frac{36}{1}$, and makes 6^2, $\sqrt{36}$, $\frac{36}{6} \div \frac{6}{1}$, and $10^3 \times 10^3$ almost inaccessible. The result: math anxiety and an "I can't" attitude.

2. *Mislearned information:* Learning facts, such as the times tables, without really understanding them can result in mislearning or learning inaccuracies. For example, the student who sees 36 as a magic solution to 6×6 rather than as the simple result of adding six sixes is open to learning errors, such as 6×6 equals, not 36, but 32. Once this error is learned and repeated over and over again, it will lead to additional errors:

$$\frac{32}{6} = 6, \quad 6\overset{60}{\overline{)320}}, \quad \frac{32}{6} + 2 = 8$$

and ultimately to math anxiety.

3. *Mismatched teaching strategies and learning readiness:* I will deal with this topic in greater detail in Chapter 6, "Matching Instruction to Cognitive Levels," but for now we can look at a case study of a child in an accelerated kindergarten program. The child is four years old and is able to count to 100; order objects in a series from smallest to largest; and group objects by shape, color, and size. Impressed by these accomplishments, the child's parents introduce her to written numerals and basic arithmetic via boxed flash cards. Because the child's cognitive development is not ready to equate written symbols with numbers or to make the logical connections required for addition and subtraction, she feels distress and learns to dislike numbers.

Math Anxiety and the Affective Domain

The affective domain of learning is its emotional component. This is the province of attitudes about learning math, of memories of past failures and successes, of influences from math-anxious or math-confident adults, of responses to the learning environment and teaching styles. The affective domain provides a context for learning. If the affective domain provides a positive context, children can be motivated to learn, whatever their math aptitude. If the affective domain provides a negative context, even children with superior math-learning ability may develop math anxiety.

Since children will have different aptitudes, teachers often think in terms of a basic, compensatory formula (this formula is not a mathematical formula in the sense of being derived from proof but, rather, a way to conceptualize a difficult, emotionally laden construct):

$$\text{aptitude} \times \text{effort} \times \text{intervention} = \text{achievement}$$

To reach the class goals for achievement, students with high ability will require less work and less intervention in the form of tutoring or special assignments than students with less ability. For example, if aptitude is rated on a scale from 1 to 12, students of aptitude level 3 will need to do twice as much work and receive twice as much intervention to reach achievement level 12 as will students whose aptitude level is already 12.

If we add the affective domain to the formula, it still works for the plus side of the equation. Positive influences from the affective domain might be equated with multiplying the whole by a positive number: the greater the number, the greater the final amount. For the minus side, the math-anxious student, however, everything changes. As with multiplying with a negative number, negative influences from the cognitive domain can actually reverse gains. More math homework and more intervention may in fact lead to lower achievement as anxiety levels increase, and some of the most anxious students in my math classes have been those with the greatest aptitude.

Learning associated with the affective domain proceeds primarily by *conditioning* and takes place largely at an unconscious level. An element of this learning is on the order of knee-jerk reactions. An obviously negative stimulus, such as a fifty-problem math test, elicits a predictably negative response, such as distaste or dread. Other conditioning patterns are less predictable. We have all heard of Pavlov's dogs. By repeatedly ringing a bell prior to feeding the dogs, Pavlov conditioned the dogs to associate bell ringing with food. Salivating, the dog's natural response to the smell and taste of food, then became linked to the sound of the bell ringing: when the dogs heard the bell, they would begin to salivate. After this association was formed, the salivation would occur even in the absence of food.

The keys are *association* and *repetition*. I once observed a math teacher who used a pointer like a whip throughout the lesson. He jabbed at the board, emphasized points with sharp whacks, and underscored class discussion by beating a tattoo on his desk. The teacher saw the pointer as his attention getter and keeper: "No one falls asleep in my class." The students did pay attention, but many of them winced repeatedly throughout the class. At an emotional level, the teacher was conditioning the students to associate math with a symbolic whipping.

Other conditioned patterns might include associating math learning with punishment or failure with fear (either one's own or others'), or with unpleasantness—the bitter pill we have to take, the tedious chore we must do before we can play, the price we have to pay, the punishment we have to endure. In each case, the associated emotion has nothing to do with math itself, but repeated experiences make the connection habitual.

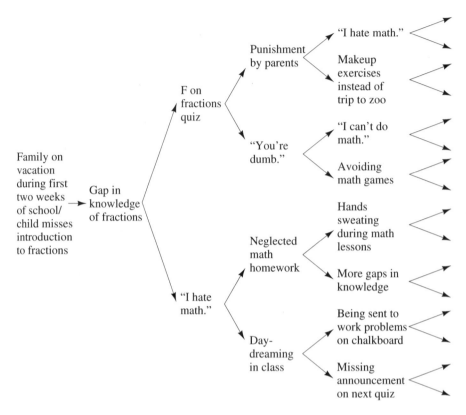

FIGURE 1-3   Math-Anxiety Chain Reaction

Math Anxiety and Affective–Cognitive Interactions

Given the potential for both affective and cognitive factors to produce math anxiety, is it accurate to talk about cognitive math anxiety and affective math anxiety? Not really. Although the initial impetus for the anxiety may come from either domain, the construct weaves them together in a stimulus–response chain reaction. Figure 1-3 above illustrates.

Of course, not every learning problem will set off a math-anxiety chain reaction. Physicists talk about a critical mass that must be present before a reaction becomes self-sustaining. With math anxiety, critical mass is probably the point at which negative influences and reactions outweigh the positive.

Once started, a math-anxiety chain reaction is difficult to stop and even more difficult to reverse. For this reason, preventive measures outperform therapies in building math confidence. However, whether you are attempting to prevent or to cure math anxiety, keep these key points in mind:

1. Math anxiety is not just a simple nervous reaction, nor is it a harmless myth: it is a debilitating affliction that restricts math performance among both children and adults, worldwide.
2. Because the math-anxiety construct spans both the affective and cognitive domains of learning, treatment must include both affective and cognitive elements.
3. No one is "math-dumb." Everyone—whether primarily "right-brained" or "left-brained," mathematically gifted or mathematically challenged—can learn math and enjoy numbers.

Questions for Thought and Discussion

1. Is becoming math anxious an inevitable part of learning math? What types of learning experiences might foster anxiety? Are these experiences usual or unusual?
2. Is your math learning more logical or more emotional? Which factors in your learning belong to the affective domain and which factors to the cognitive domain?
3. Have you ever experienced an anxiety chain reaction? What started it? What stopped it, or did it keep going?
4. How would you respond to the teacher comments quoted at the beginning of the chapter? Do you agree with any of them? Why or why not?

Activities

1. Use the problem-solving process illustrated in Figure 1-1 to diagram your working of the following problem: 18 ÷ ½. Be sure to include both cognitive and affective factors in your diagram.
2. Identify a knowledge gap or a negative attitude in your own math background or that of someone you know. Then, working backward, try to unravel the various causes and effects that produced the deficiency.

Annotated List of Readings

McCleod, Douglas B., and Verna M. Adams, eds. *Affect and Mathematical Problem-Solving: A New Perspective.* New York: Springer-Verlag, 1989. *A series of essays exploring math affect and problem solving. Covers definitions, relevant issues, and critical research.*

Mayer, Richard. E. *Thinking, Problem Solving, Cognition,* 2nd ed. New York: W. H. Freeman, 1992. *A readable overview of existing theories and models of problem solving.*

2

Diagnosing the Math-Anxious Teacher

Most math anxiety is learned at a very early age—often in elementary school, sometimes even in kindergarten. Preventing math anxiety, then, must begin with the elementary school teacher. Unfortunately, many arithmetic teachers are themselves math anxious. They may feel uncomfortable with fractions or decimals, become confused when they attempt to explain practical applications, or simply dislike numbers. Whatever the symptom, left untreated, those anxieties may not only grow, but they may also infect another generation of students. Math-anxious teachers produce math-anxious students, and helping teachers confront and control their own fears and feelings of insecurity when faced with numbers is essential if we are to stop the spread of the disease.

Modeling Math Anxiety

What happens when a math-anxious teacher attempts to teach arithmetic? First, we need to distinguish between the overt lesson—the actual subject matter being taught—and the covert lesson—the complex system of attitudes and strategies for coping with the subject matter that the teacher demonstrates in the course of his or her teaching. The overt lesson may be well planned and well explained. In fact, it may repeat word for word the lesson of an unanxious teacher. However, if the covert lesson shows anxiety, even controlled anxiety, the class will tend to learn the anxiety with or even instead of the concepts.

This is particularly true for elementary school children. In a later chapter we will look at the nature of learning during various stages of development, but for the moment we can focus on one important characteristic of early learning: imitation. Elementary school children are also empiricists. Their physical senses are their touchstones—their tests of value—and also the anchors for their thought patterns. Consequently, they have a heightened sensitivity to physical stimuli: they will "see" the strain behind a smile or "hear" tension in a voice. If there is a discrepancy between the lesson the teacher speaks and the lesson the teacher shows, they will sense that too. When children demonstrate what they have learned, they will imitate the unconscious as well as the conscious lesson. Repeatedly observing and imitating mathematical procedures and anxious behaviors together establish a learning pattern that is difficult to break.

The overall learning process at work here is what social-learning theorists refer to as vicarious learning: learning through observation. When a behavior is modeled, an observer learns the behavior, then imitates or attempts to imitate the behavior. If the modeled behavior is positive, the results will generally be positive. If the modeled behavior is negative, so will be the results. And if the behavior modeled incorporates a mixture of positive and negative behaviors, the results will generally be mixed. For example, a teacher who hates math may teach students to despise multiplying or dividing, even if they understand the concepts. And a teacher who feels insecure working with numbers will communicate that insecurity, even when teaching the simplest procedures.

To teach math successfully, the teacher must also be a good math model. In other words, what the teacher says about math and what the teacher feels about math must match.

Teacher's Math Anxiety Self-Quiz

Who is math anxious? All teachers? Most teachers? Only the cursed few? Many math-anxious teachers feel they are alone in their problem, but my own studies of teacher trainees suggest the problem is both widespread and deeply entrenched. The Math Anxiety Self-Quiz in Figure 2-1 (page 12) offers a simple way to rate individual anxiety levels.

Among the hundreds of students who have taken the quiz, most give more *yes* than *no* responses. For some, recognizing their math anxiety is a surprise; they had looked only at individual reactions—discomfort with fractions or graphs, preferences for art or history—rather than at the anti-math pattern of those reactions. For others, the quiz simply reaffirms something they have known for years.

My treatment for these teacher trainees combines techniques of counseling therapy with liberal doses of mathematics instruction. In each case, however, I counsel patience. Just as math anxiety is not developed overnight, math confidence will not be achieved in a day, a week, or a month.

FIGURE 2-1   Teachers' Math Anxiety Self-Quiz

Answer each of the following questions *yes* or *no* by making an X in the appropriate column. Work quickly, giving your first spontaneous responses.

	Yes	*No*
1. Do you dislike working with numbers?	____	____
2. Do you dislike reading graphs or charts?	____	____
3. Have you ever had trouble with a math class?	____	____
4. Do you consider yourself to be verbal rather than quantitative—a word person rather than a numbers person?	____	____
5. Would you rather give your students a lesson in history or art than an arithmetic lesson?	____	____
6. Would explaining fractions or decimals to a grade school class be difficult for you?	____	____
7. If you worked an arithmetic problem and got an answer different from the one in the book, would you assume the mistake was yours?	____	____
8. Do you perspire or does your heart beat increase when you take a math test?	____	____
9. Do you believe that people who are good at math were born with that ability?	____	____
10. Have you ever avoided taking a math class?	____	____

Add up the numbers of *yes* and *no* responses. If there are more *yes* than *no* responses, you may be math anxious. The greater the number of *yes* responses, the greater the chance of your being math anxious.

Source: Reprinted with permission from Joseph G. R. Martinez, "Preventing Math Anxiety: A Prescription," *Academic Therapy, 23,* (November 1987); p. 119.

Self-Disclosure

As with any negative behavior, effecting a change must begin with admitting that there is in fact a problem. Some teachers and teacher education students will not admit to being math anxious. "I simply do not like math," they will say, or, "Numbers are dehumanizing; I'm not a numbers person," or even, "Math is not my best subject. I'm verbal, not quantitative."

Helping these people admit and confront their fears is a crucial first step. Small-group discussions in a semiprivate but informal setting such as an office or teachers' lounge provide a supportive forum for self-disclosure. A discussion facilitator initiates and sets the tone for the discussion, then adds questions or comments whenever necessary to encourage participants to talk through their own feelings. A discussion with a group of teachers or student teachers might go something like this:

Facilitator: What I enjoyed most about grade school math was doing problems in my head. I hated it, though, when Sister Catherine would send us to the board. I'd write as small as I could and keep my back to the class.

Participant A: I didn't mind going to the board, but I'd freeze if the teacher said, "Multiply five times five, then divide by five, and subtract two."

Facilitator: You must have felt confident, though, if you didn't mind doing problems on the board.

Participant A: Well, usually there would be several of us working problems at the same time, so no one would be watching just me.

Participant B: Then you really weren't so confident after all if you needed to hide in a crowd.

Participant A: I guess that's true. I never really liked math.

Discussion of the Math Anxiety Self-Quiz can also provide a take-off exercise for self-disclosure. Probing the why's behind each *yes* answer often results in statements that begin with "I'm afraid." For example, asked why they dislike working with numbers, teachers or trainees reply, "I'm afraid of making mistakes" or "I'm afraid to try." Asked why they would rather give a lesson in art or history than in arithmetic, they say, "I'm afraid of looking dumb."

Once anxieties have been brought out in the open, causes—the events, circumstances, or combination of factors that led to the feelings—may be explored. In some cases a negative attitude will be linked to a particular teacher—"Mrs. Kennedy taught math, and she never liked me"—or to a particular class—"All my problems started in the fourth grade when I had the mumps and got behind." In other cases, there may be no identifiable time, place, or person but, rather, a vague sense of uneasiness about math that developed over a period of years. Women particularly may recall feeling at an early age that girls are not or even should not be good at math—an attitude that can be traced to multiple causes, including home influences.

"Writing the problem"—exploring math memories and behaviors on paper—is an effective way to get at forgotten or buried causes of math anxiety. The following examples are from the learning journals of several math-anxious teacher trainees.

Student Teacher #1

Initially I had a difficult time remembering whether there was anything significant about my experiences with math. Nothing came to mind, or I had never processed my reactions to my math classes. Yet clearly I can recall the time or period when math became a class that I feared. It was during my early school years. I specifically recall being placed in an advanced math group. Being only one of the few minority students is what I recall vividly. I immediately felt intimidated and believed I could not compete with others because of minority status. This is something I had not realized until now.

Student Teacher #2

I should here remark on my troubled math past, involving tears, tutors, and despair. School had always been easy and instinctive. I was a very creative kid with "potential," which also suggests laziness. Straight "A's" in every subject 'cept for math. Thus began my feelings of ineptitude and real stupidity, which was my secret.

Student Teacher #3

I have always felt that math was incomprehensible and have a lot of anxiety about it. My father was an economist, and a lot of our battles were over my math problems as I remember. What was very clear to him was absolutely overwhelming to me. Sometimes my brain just locks and I can't put in one more piece of information. I am alarmed at the number of mistakes in arithmetic I make. A problem since the second grade.

Student Teacher #4

Interesting observation about working with Jim, my math tutor, in a one-on-one session. When we were working at the table, and I felt safe with my rules and notebook, etc., I wasn't anxious about responding to his questions about how I was working certain problems. But when he asked me to do one on the blackboard, I went to the board and *froze*. I could feel myself dissociating, actually "losing my mind" for a moment. The problem was scrambled; I wasn't able to work it; I looked to him for help. When I sat down I was chagrined and disappointed in myself. Was it because he was a man that I got anxious? Or because I was at the blackboard? Both?

After giving it some thought, I believe that there are several things operating here in my anxiety (which was intense enough to cause me to dissociate): first of all, going to the blackboard has old associations with the nuns. When one was called in front of the room to do something on the board, it was almost always as a punishment. Blackboards are associated with shaming behaviors. Not surprising that this old material compounded my math anxiety. Secondly, I was chagrined at myself for looking to Jim for help when I felt lost. I thought, in retrospect, that this was a regression to a socialized bottom-line point where I was anxious enough to have regressed to the safety of dominant/submissive, male/female gender roles. . . . Math anxiety compounded by performance anxiety = defense mechanisms alert: regression and dissociation. Seems too tidy to be true, but since I experienced it, I believe I'm on target here.

The first three student teachers discuss their math anxieties in general; the fourth focuses on a specific "attack" of anxiety and its effect on performance. In each case, the anxiety emerges from a complex system of social and learning conditions. Student teacher #1, a Native American, was intimidated by being placed in an advanced math group with nonminority students—a promotion that her teacher probably intended as recogniton for superior ability in math. Student teacher #3 tied math anxiety to an intimidating authority figure and to some unidentified problem with arithmetic in the second grade. And student teacher #4 traced her anxiey attack to grade school punishments and gender stereotypes.

Later in this chapter we will look at the individual strategies these student teachers developed to cope with their anxieties. Although the special configuration of distressing influences differs for each person, there is nonetheless some common ground. All four trace their anxieties to grade school. All four had buried their anxieties emotionally and intellectually, either denying or rationalizing them. Three of the four linked their problems with math to societal pressures external to the subject matter—an authoritarian parent and teachers, restrictive gender stereotypes, and ethnic identity. Two identified math itself as a problem, although one of the two linked the incomprehensibiity of math to arguments with a math-proficient father. And all four displayed similar effects: self-disparagement, avoidance of all math-related activities, some dissociation when faced with a problem they could not master immediately, and physical symptoms of distress (increased rates in heartbeat and respiration, dry mouth, damp hands, and so forth).

Strategies for Coping with Math-Anxious Behaviors and Feelings

Controlling math-anxious behaviors is not enough; math-anxious feelings must also be controlled. I know one spartan math teacher who views math as one of those unpleasant facts of life. He tells his students, "You don't have to like it; just do it." His classes have a bite-the-bullet character that shadows learning with gloom. Another math teacher constantly "proves" her proficiency by aiming her lessons above her students' level. Both teachers are themselves math anxious. Both have confronted their fears head on by becoming math teachers. But neither has dealt with personal anxieties about math; consequently, neither is a good math teacher and each unconsciously propagates negative attitudes about math learning.

Successfully coping with math anxiety calls for attacking the problem both inside and outside. The strategies listed here have been particularly effective for teachers and teacher trainees, but the methods will work equally well for those pursuing other careers.

1. *Understanding the individual problem:* What are the dimensions of math anxiety? Are all math anxieties the same? Is math anxiety an all-or-nothing disease? That is, is it possible to be anxious about some math topics but not about others?

When we say someone is math anxious, we are actually describing the symptoms rather than the causes. As we saw with the four student teachers, the original causes of math anxiety are as diverse as the individuals themselves. Similarly, the specific insecurities or learning gaps that currently trigger the symptoms may vary from person to person.

Understanding one's own math anxieties should begin with defining what they are and what they are not. A person who says, "I hate numbers," may find on further reflection that he or she hates specific types of numbers—fractions, negative numbers, percentages—or hates numbers in specific contexts—word problems, bank balances, income tax forms. Developing a math-anxiety profile enables individuals to explore and chart their own math anxieties. A test that links math knowledge and feelings about that knowledge provides data for a profile that encompasses the cognitive and the affective domains of math anxiety. The Math Problems and Mini-Math Anxiety Scale (classroom tested with students from grade school to college) in Figure 2-2 below provided the data for the profile of one teacher trainee in Figures 2-3(a) and 2-3(b) on page 19.

FIGURE 2-2   Math Problems and Mini–Math Anxiety Scale (Martinez, Joseph G. R., 1992)

General Directions:

Without the use of a calculator, follow specific directions and work each problem. Also, for each problem, Circle Y for Yes or N for No to the question: Does this problem make you anxious? Please respond spontaneously to this question. Good luck!

1. Y N   12
             9
           +15

2. Y N   124
             68
           +39

3. Y N   −28
             12
            −13

4. Y N $-8 + 24 + (-12) =$

5. Y N $16 \times 3 =$

6. Y N   121
           × 11

7. Y N $\dfrac{124}{4} =$

8. Y N $215 \div 5 =$

9. Y N $13^2 =$

Continued

FIGURE 2-2 *Continued*

10. Y N $6^4 =$

11. Y N $\sqrt{121} =$

12. Y N $\sqrt{256} =$

13. Y N $\dfrac{1}{8} + \dfrac{1}{5} =$

14. Y N $\dfrac{3}{4} + 1\dfrac{1}{2} =$

15. Y N $\dfrac{1}{3} - \dfrac{1}{10} =$

16. Y N $1\dfrac{7}{8} - \dfrac{3}{4} =$

17. Y N $\dfrac{5}{10} \times \dfrac{4}{25} =$

18. Y N $\dfrac{150}{49} \times \dfrac{7}{15} \times \dfrac{2}{10} =$

19. Y N $\dfrac{1}{8} \div 3 =$

20. Y N $\dfrac{12}{144} \div \dfrac{1}{4} =$

21. Y N $(1/3)^2$

23. Y N $\sqrt{\dfrac{84}{21}} =$

22. Y N $(4/5)^3 =$

24. Y N $\sqrt{\dfrac{1}{3} \times \dfrac{27}{1}} =$

25. Y N $6.2 + 4.8 =$

26. Y N $.012 + .1005 =$

27. Y N $3.01 - 3.001 =$

28. Y N $-2.5 + 7.06 =$

29. Y N $4.1 \times 3.2 =$

30. Y N $13.6 \times .012 =$

31. Y N $1.19 \div .7 =$

32. Y N $\dfrac{.168}{.014} =$

33. Y N $(1.5)^2 =$

34. Y N $(.03)^2 =$

35. Y N $\sqrt{.0064} =$

36. Y N $\sqrt{.0289} =$

37. Y N Find the perimeter of the rectangle: 6″ 8″

38. Y N Find the hypotenuse of the rectangle in #37.

39. Y N If 1″ were subtracted from each side of the rectangle in #37, what would the hypotenuse be? (Approximate)

Continued

FIGURE 2-2   *Continued*

40. Y   N   If 1″ were subtracted from the hypotenuse and from the 6″ width in #37, what would the length be? (Approximate)

41. Y   N   Find the area of a circle whose radius is 7″.

42. Y   N   Find the area of a triangle whose base is 6″ and whose height = 3″.

43. Y   N   Divide the radius in problem #41 by two; then determine the area.

44. Y   N   Divide the base in problem #42 by 3; then find the area.

45. Y   N   Find the area of a square whose side = 5″.

46. Y   N   What is the volume of a cube whose height = 1 foot, length = 1 foot, and width = 1 foot?

47. Y   N   Find the square root of your answer to problem #45.

48. Y   N   Find the cube root of your answer for problem #46.

Solve for x in problems 49–60:

49. Y   N $2x + 4 = 16$

50. Y   N $2x + 4 = 16 + x$

51. Y   N $-x = 1$

52. Y   N $-2x + 4 = 16$

53. Y   N $2(x + 4) = 16$

54. Y   N $4(x + 2) = 3x$

55. Y   N $\dfrac{1}{x} = \dfrac{1}{2}$

56. Y   N $\dfrac{1}{x} = \dfrac{1}{a} + \dfrac{1}{b}$

57. Y   N $x^2 = 4$

58. Y   N $2x^2 = 50$

59. Y   N $\sqrt{x^2} =$

60. Y   N $\sqrt{4x^2}$

61. Y   N   What number plus five is twenty-one?

62. Y   N   What number is ten more than six?

63. Y   N   What number is ten less than twenty-eight?

64. Y   N   What number minus ten is forty-seven?

Continued

FIGURE 2-2   *Continued*

65. Y N	Two-thirds of what number is forty-eight?	66. Y N One-fifth of what number is sixty-nine?
67. Y N	What number divided by six is one-half?	68. Y N What number divided by eight is sixteen?
69. Y N	The square of what number is one hundred twenty-one?	70. Y N The cube of what number is eight?
71. Y N	The square root of two hundred twenty-five is what number?	72. Y N The cube root of one hundred twenty-five is what number?

Source: Joseph G. R. Martinez (1992).

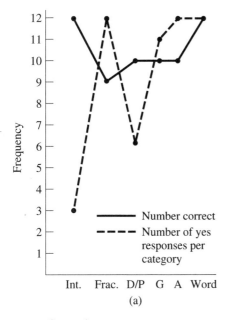

(a)

Categories:

Int. = Integers
Frac. = Fractions
D/P = Decimals/percents
G = Geometry
A = Algebra
Word = Word problems

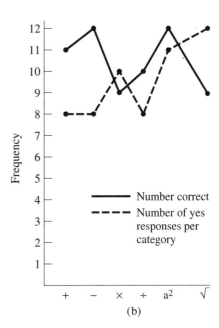

(b)

Operations:

+ = Addition
− = Subtraction
× = Multiplication
÷ = Division
a^2 = Exponents
$\sqrt{}$ = Roots (square, cube)

FIGURE 2-3   Math-Anxiety Profile

Although he had few anxieties about integers and some anxiety about decimals and percentages, the student showed high anxiety about fractions, geometry, algebra, word problems, and working with exponents and roots. The anxiety profile shows not only gaps in knowledge but also anxieties about most math problems that go beyond simple operations with integers. In fact, although his answers were correct for the word problems, he circled all of them, indicating feelings of high anxiety.

2. *Making a plan of action:* Once the specific parameters of the problem are defined, it is time for a plan of action. If a discovery exercise (such as the preceding profile activity) suggests gaps in knowledge, taking a basic math course might be a good starting place. If the gaps in knowledge are few but the anxieties many, the plan might include desensitizing activities or use of behavior modification with a carefully charted chain of behaviors and reinforcements, as in the Math Self-Change Project outlined in the Appendix.

Each identified component of anxiety requires a response. If analysis points toward both knowledge of and attitude about fractions, the plan should tackle both domains of the problem. For example, knowledge of fractions can be improved by using a computer tutorial program or by taking a class or workshop. Negative attitudes about fractions can be altered by systematic work and reinforcement—by, in effect, developing the habit of liking fractions. On the other hand, if analysis shows no gaps in knowledge, only a strong antipathy for fractions, then the action might involve conditioning positive feelings to accompany the behavior—such as linking fractions to feelings of pleasure by repeatedly doing problems involving fractions while listening to some favorite music or enjoying a fire in the fireplace or sipping a favorite coffee.

3. *Relearning and overlearning:* Because a key component of anxiety is insecurity, becoming confident about math is essential. Relearning elementary-level math from an adult's perspective can be a surprisingly gratifying experience. Memories of learning nightmares are frozen in time. They will retain the taste of defeat and struggle long after the reason for the problem is past. Third-graders might struggle with long division because the concept or the teaching method does not match their intellectual development (see Chapter 6 for more about matching tasks, pedagogy, and development). An adult may remember long division as being too difficult; but in relearning long division in a class or personal study, the adult, whose intellectual development far exceeds the requirements of all basic math concepts, will usually excel. The general effect is to substitute a positive for a negative learning experience. Moreover, the adult's sense of accomplishment often exceeds that of a youngster who has mastered the same procedure; as the years of anxiety have magnified the problem, they also magnify the victory.

As they relearn, most adults will tend to overlearn as well. That works for them in at least two major ways. First, overlearning involves devoting extra time to studying math, and the greater the time and the greater the frequency of study, the less intimidating it will be. Second, overlearning builds confidence—a feeling of "owning" the knowledge and an accompanying pride in that ownership.

4. *Thinking about learning—The metacognitive approach:* Becoming math anxious is insidious; before victims realize what is happening, they are experiencing symptoms. But becoming math confident requires direct, conscious action. The metacognitive approach calls for the math-anxious to understand, plan, and manage their own recovery. All the coping strategies I have outlined here have a metacognitive component, but the metacognitive approach takes us a step further. *Metacognition* means thinking about thinking. Thus, taking a metacognitive approach to math anxiety means analyzing thought processes about math; translating anxieties about math into thoughts and then analyzing those thoughts; and systematically monitoring and analyzing math-related behaviors over an extended period of time. Literally, the approach calls for becoming immersed in math and in the process of math learning.

The Math Learning Journal

When I use this approach with math-anxious teacher trainees, I have them keep a math learning journal. At the beginning of the activity, their daily entries usually focus on anxieties, primarily how they feel about the day's math homework. For example, the following entries are from the first two weeks of a trainee's learning journal:

> *Day #1:* I am scared that even with the help of a tutor and study group, I won't be able to pass math and that will end the pursuit of my degree. I have put this class off as long as I could.

> *Day #7:* I was doing the exercises in the book and ran into some difficulty and asked someone who I knew had taken a lot of math for help. The memories of why I dislike math so much came back to me when she said, "What do you mean you don't understand this? It's *so* simple."

As the weeks progress, entries become increasingly analytical and begin to focus on solving the problem rather than simply rehearsing it.

> *Day #25:* I need to write important rules and formulas as I encounter them and not wait till the end of the chapter or the night before the test. I need to anticipate and not simply react.

> *Day #32:* Today I made myself come to the library to study. It was a good decision for me because I found that I could concentrate more and had less distractions. I kept with it and I slowly began to understand what had confused me so much before. I need to give myself time and not think that

just because I didn't get it the first time around does not mean that I'll never get it.

Toward the end of the journal, the trainee emphasizes accomplishment and a growing sense of confidence.

Day #60: A few weeks ago I never thought I could learn the concepts in math; and now I am learning them and recognizing when an error is made. Who would have thought such a thing was possible?

Day #72: I got my test back and I got an 88%. I am ready for this class to be over and yet I will miss the challenge of learning a new concept and being able to do it later on an exam. This class has really done a lot for my ego. I was terrified and I made it with a better grade than merely passing.

The success of the metacognitive method depends greatly on what one of my students calls "letting my math anxiety work for me." As with using biofeedback techniques to deal with various physical or emotional problems, this student watches for math-anxiety symptoms. They are, she says, "like buzzers going off in my head telling me it's time for more intervention or for more positive self-reinforcement." Significantly, for many students an early warning is the denial of math anxiety. Denying anxiety while experiencing its effects often short-circuits a timely, effective response. By the time the anxiety forces its way to the surface, the problem is out of control.

Case Studies

Which strategy or strategies will work best depends on numerous factors: the causes of the anxiety, the degree of anxiety, the length of time the person has suffered from it. A relatively mild case of short duration might be dealt with in a few workshops or awareness activities. However, a severe case of many years' duration (and many teachers' or teacher trainees' anxiety has plagued them since elementary school) will require more extensive treatment.

The four teacher trainees whom I mentioned earlier in this chapter experienced math anxiety at levels that on a scale of 1 to 10 could be rated 5 and above, with trainee #4 the most anxious and trainee #2 the least anxious. Each trainee developed and implemented a plan to cope with math anxiety; the success of the plans seemed to depend less on the initial intensity of the anxiety itself than on the scope and intensity of the effort to deal with the problem.

Coping with Math Anxiety Case Study:
Student Teacher #1

Student teacher #1 began with a dislike for math but denied feeling math anxiety. After both oral and written activities to discover why she disliked math, she realized that she felt insecure in math classes and recalled her experiences as a minority student in an advanced class. Although the root cause of her anxieties was social rather than cognitive, the student teacher found she had developed some poor math-learning habits. She tended to quit listening in class when she felt under pressure, to quit trying when a problem became difficult, and to do less rather than more math as the material increased in complexity.

The student teacher's plan of action began with taking a math class. She developed a technique she called "self-talk" for recalling her attention to math. She also practiced doing problems in her head to develop her math "muscles." And because her preference for working alone seemed to promote hours of elaborate math-avoidance schemes, she engaged a tutor to help her focus on and stick to the subject.

The student teacher's records show a steady increase in time devoted to math studies and an increasing confidence in her knowledge. However, she did not make equal progress in learning to like and enjoy math.

Coping with Math Anxiety Case Study:
Student Teacher #2

The second student teacher began his coping exercise by quoting a professor who called him "the epitome of the underachiever" and a master of the "fuzzy studies" that involve reading and writing. A self-disclosure exercise revealed that he had always had a secret fear that he was stupid in math, a fear that had been reinforced by the ease with which he grasped verbal studies and the struggle he had with math. His defense mechanisms included self-ridicule (he called his "troubled past" with mathematics a saga of pain, misery, and *real* stupidity) and lazy study habits that provided an excuse for poor performance ("I can't be expected to know something I didn't study").

In addition to taking a math class, the student teacher kept a learning journal, which he used primarily for catharsis. Entries consist of negative memories about past experiences with math, diatribes about current struggles (all liberally sprinkled with four-letter words), and excuses for continuing to avoid serious math study (too much stress from tests, not enough time, a preference for writing songs or attending parties).

This attack-and-abuse method had only limited success. The student teacher turned his fear into anger and then coped successfully with the material, achieving an "A" in his math course. At the same time, however, he developed an almost savage attitude toward math that suggests his basic anxieties were simply buried deeper rather than dealt with directly.

Coping with Math Anxiety Case Study: Student Teacher #3

Student teacher #3 mixed feelings of low self-esteem with an often-repeated conviction that math was incomprehensible. Her self-disclosure activity pointed toward problems with an authoritarian, math-proficient father and discovered subtle, unconscious ploys to make math study impossible—for example, losing her glasses when she changed planes so that she could not continue to study math on the next flight, or scheduling other activities during math class.

The student teacher kept a learning journal of her progress in a math class. Entries for the first few weeks of class are riddled with variations on two themes: "I don't understand" and "Why? Why? Why?" At midterm she added tutoring sessions to her plan of action and directed her "why" questions to the tutor. The number and intensity of the negative comments then decreased, replaced by an increasing number of positive reports—good grades on tests, pleased surprise at understanding a difficult concept, reports of intense but successful study sessions.

At the beginning of the exercise, the student teacher had written, "I'm overwhelmed and it's not fun." Toward the end, she wrote, "I have enjoyed the classes and am pleased I have done well. . . . I know I'm capable." She describes a tutoring session in which she was too involved in doing the problems to pay attention to a fire alarm: "Burning seemed better than interrupting the pursuit of the elusive number."

Coping with Math Anxiety Case Study: Student Teacher #4

The fourth student teacher, according to her own analysis, was so math anxious that she would literally "lose" her mind when faced with math. Exploring her past, she discovered that she had been socialized to dislike math (girls do not like math, do not do well in math, do not need to know math as wives or nuns, etc.). She also discovered a link in her memories between learning math and being punished or publicly shamed.

Deciding that she needed to countersocialize herself as well as learn the math she missed during her growing-up years, the student teacher planned an intensive summer of metacognitive therapy—four weeks of tutoring and study group preparation, then a four-week advanced math course. Throughout the period, she devoted four to six hours a day to studying math, then fifteen minutes to half an hour a day to her learning journal.

At the beginning of the eight weeks, she devoted several sessions to examining past experiences. She discovered a tendency to overintellectualize her anxieties as well as a tendency to exaggerate her problems with learning math. Realizing that she usually would begin to discuss her math anxiety by referring to herself as "the girl who failed high school algebra," she looked up her high school transcripts and found she had not failed after all: she passed with a respectable "C." She also found that her study group had a tendency to reinforce her anxieties since the members spent too much time trading and sympathizing with each other's fears; therefore, she placed a moratorium on "pity parties" and tried to make a distinction between analyzing anxieties and indulging them.

Overlearning was an important part of the student teacher's strategy. After the first test in her math class, she wrote, "Not as anxious as I ought to be! The relative 'calm' comes I think from knowing that I've tried *almost* as hard as I can; I know *most* of what I need; and I'm aware of my limitations (math errors; forgetting or misapplying rules, etc.)." A week later she returned to overintellectualizing, this time wondering why she was *not* feeling anxiety: "It feels like something must be wrong because this test I'm preparing for seems easier than the others. So what am I missing? Could it be that I'm not missing *anything* but that I'm understanding the material?" At one point she undermined her own progress by deciding that the next test would determine whether she had the "right stuff," but she received a nearly perfect score despite the extra, self-imposed stress and decided, "I *am* going to make it!"

By the end of the math course, the student teacher felt burned out and was somewhat worried about retaining the information and attitudes, but on the whole felt "competent to do the work, not too anxious, just a little curious about the methods."

Summary of the Case Studies

Of the four student teachers, the first two were least successful in dealing with their anxieties and the last two most successful. However, all four made positive strides. Number one began to develop some study habits that should eventually lead to math confidence. Number two substituted some positive for some negative learning experiences. Number three showed the beginnings of a real interest in math as a subject. And number four countered a lifetime of negative attitudes and experiences with a crash course in math confidence that literally developed new thinking and learning patterns.

Can we say that any of these student teachers has been cured of math anxiety? Probably not. But each of them has taken a step toward control over anxiety, and three of the four have begun to reverse the complex process that made them math-anxious adults.

Questions for Thought and Discussion

1. Why do so many teachers suffer from math anxiety? How might colleges help to remedy the problem?
2. Have you ever studied math with a math-anxious teacher? An anxiety-producing teacher?
3. Who was your best math teacher? Your worst? What made them good or bad? What lasting effects did they have on your math learning?
4. What characteristics or behaviors would make a teacher a positive math model? Have you ever studied math with such a teacher?

Activities

1. *Math Learning Journal:* Enroll in a math course or develop a plan for self-study. Then examine your experiences in daily journal entries. Try to get past the surface of the problem and explore the why's of your reactions. Experiment with various solutions to negative experiences or attitudes and record the results.
2. *Math Self-Change Project:* See the appendix.

Annotated List of Readings

Tobias, Sheila. *Succeed with Math.* New York: College Board, 1987. *Extension of earlier study with special attention to "reading" mathematics in the various disciplines.*

Zaslavsky, Claudia. *Fear of Math: How to Get over It and Get On with Your Life.* New Brunswick, NJ: Rutgers University Press, 1994. *Multicultural approach to understanding math learning and overcoming math anxiety. Explores math phobia by explicating sociological dimensions of the issue. Explodes myths and stereotypes.*

3

---

*Avoiding
Math-Anxious Teaching*

Consider the following classroom scenarios:

Scenario #1

A class of fifth-graders sits in rows of desks facing a chalkboard. On each desk are an exercise sheet and a #2 pencil (no calculators allowed).

A teacher, armed with a pointer and a chalkholder with a long piece of yellow chalk, walks to the board and writes:

$$1/4 + 1/2 =$$

Still facing the chalkboard, he explains in a monotone: "Adding fractions is easy. First, find the lowest common denominator. Second, add the numerators. And you have it: the answer is three-fourths."

In the back row, a student leans toward her neighbor and whispers, "How did he do that?"

The teacher turns quickly and jabs the pointer in her direction: "You, Miss Silva, come to the board and show us homework problem number 6: 1/3 + 2/6. Move quickly now. Write clearly and be ready to explain your answer."

Scenario #2

A group of second-graders are sitting in a circle with their teacher. In front of them are stacks of construction paper circles in various sizes that they have just finished cutting.

The teacher, who has participated in the cutting, says, "That was the easy part. Now comes the hard part—math."

The children groan in protest, but their attention remains fixed on the teacher. He picks up a large circle, folds it in half, and cuts along the fold.

"Today we're going to learn about fractions."

Another groan.

"When I cut this circle in two, does that give me two circles?"

The children, catching the word *two,* jump to a conclusion and nod, "Yes."

The teacher holds up the halves of the circle he cut and asks, "Does it really? Do these look like two circles to you? Come on kids; help your poor math-dumb teacher out. Remember, I flunked fractions in grade school."

The children giggle at the joke, but their eyes open wide: they can't imagine their teacher flunking anything.

Scenario #3

Small groups of fourth-graders are sitting at round tables in a classroom filled with plants and pictures but no chalkboards. Each fourth-grader has a calculator, and each group has a student leader. All of the leaders are talking at the same time, calling the groups' attention to the sets of division problems silhouetted by an overhead projector on a movie screen.

"To do division," the group leaders explain, "You first enter the number you're dividing. Then punch the division sign, the line with a dot above and below it. Then enter the number you're dividing by. Simple. 1288 divided by 14 is 92."

"I didn't get that. I got 87."

"You're dumb."

"Ms. Conroy!"

While the students work, their teacher has been moving from table to table answering questions and making comments. She appears quickly when her name is called, reproves the group leader for calling a member of the group dumb, and assures the students, "There are no dummies in this class."

The exercise continues until all the students have arrived at the same answers. Then the teacher goes to a blank board set on an easel and writes: 14 $\overline{)1288}$

"This is the old-time way to do problem number one: long division. To do long division, you have to do a lot of guessing. You have to guess how many times 14 will go into the number you're dividing. You have to multiply, too.

"Now we can see that 14 won't go into 1 at all, and it won't go into 12, so we guess that it might go into 128, maybe 8 times. Nope. 8 times 14 is 112. We'll have to try again.

"See how much work the calculator saves us, and it doesn't make mistakes either. Instead of spending all that time doing long division, you make the machine work for you."

* * * * *

Of course, Scenario #1 depicts the classic anxiety-producing math lesson. The rigid classroom arrangement, the authoritarian teacher speaking mathematicsese instead of American English, and the summons to the chalkboard—all are the elements of most math-anxious nightmares.

However, there are anxiety-producing factors in the other two scenarios as well. The teacher in Scenario #2 sits with his students on the floor and uses paper cutouts to make the lesson less threatening. At the same time, he makes math frightening. First, teaching fractions, a fifth- or sixth-grade subject, to second-graders invites confusion and an I-can't-do-it frustration (more about matching intellectual development and subject matter in Chapter 6). Second, by calling math "hard" and himself "mathdumb," he goes beyond challenging the students and makes math seem inaccessible. From the children's point of view, if their adult teacher, who knows everything about everything, flunked, what hope do they have of mastering fractions?

The small groups and peer leaders in Scenario #3 suggest that the teacher wants to empower her students to control their own math learning. Unfortunately, the students are not learning math at all: They are learning to use calculators to sidestep learning math. If their calculators fail or they are forced to work without calculators, these students will be lost. This lesson, which at the time appeared satisfactory to all concerned, may have contributed to the learning gaps that eventually trigger anxiety.

Math-anxious teaching is both a cause and an effect of math anxiety. Breaking the cycle begins, as we saw in Chapter 2, with diagnosing and treating the math-anxious teacher. While treatment is underway, the teacher can avoid math-anxious teaching by integrating compensatory strategies into lesson plans and by emphasizing the confidence-building elements of effective teaching.

Knowing the Subject/Teaching the Subject

Teacher trainees and even many veteran teachers frequently underestimate the levels of knowledge and proficiency needed to teach elementary school math. In fact, most certification programs appear to agree: if you can add, subtract, multiply, and divide; if you know something about fractions and decimals, you can successfully teach basic mathematics.

Nothing could be further from the truth. Doing-knowledge might be described as level-one knowledge: recognizing the type of problem and remembering the appropriate operations. Teaching-knowledge takes us to a higher level. It requires knowing not only the *what*'s and *how*'s but also the *why*'s .

Take, for example, the following problem:

$$\frac{1}{2} \div \frac{1}{4}$$

To do the problem, all we have to remember is a simple procedure: When dividing a fraction by a fraction, invert the fraction on the right, then multiply. To teach the problem, we have to understand *why* we invert the fraction and *why* we multiply as well as what the problem really means. Doing the problem takes three steps and a few seconds: Invert 1/4, multiply 1/2 by 4, then reduce 4/2 to get the answer 2.

Teaching the problem is more complicated. First, to help students understand the problem, we should translate math language into everyday language. The *math language* of the problem was the equation itself. In *everyday language,* the mathematical equation is asking: "How many fourths are there in one half?"

To help students "see" the problem, we might use drawings or circle cutouts, divided into halves and then into fourths. Once the students have discovered for themselves how many fourths are in a half, they are ready for a key question: When we divide by a fraction, do we increase or decrease the total number of pieces? The increase in number is, of course, the reason we invert the fraction and multiply; when students understand that, they are ready to learn the procedure. To guide students to that point, the teacher must know what it means to divide by a fraction, how to do it, and why the procedure works.

Similarly, the degree of proficiency needed to teach elementary math successfully goes beyond the level of test-taker competence. Teaching-level math proficiency calls for accuracy, speed, and the rudiments at least of math intuition—a feeling for numbers (math sense) that lets you sense whether an answer is correct or incorrect and why.

I once taught in a program that did not allow teachers to use answer books. All of us were required to work all the problems we assigned to our students. Because skills development calls for frequent repetition and constant practice, we spent hours performing the simplest operations over and over again: $12 \times 10 = 120$, $24 \times 26 = 624$, $26 \times 13 = 338$, and so forth. Moreover, because the assignments called for students to show all of their work and for us to grade the entire process, we could not take a short-cut and use our calculators. But the hours were not wasted. Every teacher developed a feeling for basic operations and a speed in performing them that made even the most hesitant into math whizzes.

Test your own proficiency with the "Teacher Tell Me Why" Test and Assessing Math Intuition exercises in Figures 3-1 below and 3-2 on page 32.

FIGURE 3-1   "Teacher Tell Me Why" Test

Answer each of the questions; then figure out a way to demonstrate the answer to your students.

1. Why do we "carry" numbers, both when we add and when we multiply?

$$
\begin{array}{rr}
4 & 1 \\
29 & 16 \\
\underline{\times\ 5} & \underline{+16} \\
145 & 32
\end{array}
$$

Continued

FIGURE 3-1 *Continued*

2. Why should we move the decimal point when we divide by numbers that contain decimals?

$$.5\overline{\smash{\big)}\,2.500} = 5.00$$

3. Why must we find a common denominator before we add or subtract fractions?

$$\frac{1}{2} - \frac{1}{6} = \frac{3}{6} - \frac{1}{6} = \frac{2}{6} = \frac{1}{3}$$

4. Why are the answers to 20^5 and 20×5 different?

5. Why do we not need to find a common denominator when we multiply or divide fractions?

$$\frac{1}{2} \times \frac{1}{2} = \frac{1}{4} \qquad \frac{1}{2} \div \frac{1}{2} = \frac{1}{2} \times \frac{2}{1} = 1$$

6. Why does the answer to a multiplication problem involving decimals move the decimal place over?

$$2.9 \times .5 = 1.45$$

7. Why does multiplying length by width give us area in square units (inches, centimeters, feet, meters, etc.)?

$$2m\ \boxed{}\ ^{4m} \qquad 2m \times 4m = 8 \text{ square meters} = 8m^2$$

8. Why does multiplying a positive number by a negative number give us a negative number?

$$-10 \times 5 = -50$$

9. Why does it work to "cancel" numbers before multiplying or dividing fractions?

$$\frac{2}{6} \times \frac{6}{2} = 1 \qquad \frac{5}{4} \div \frac{1}{4} = \frac{5}{4} \times \frac{4}{1} = 5$$

10. Why does dividing a negative number by a negative number give us a positive number?

$$\frac{-50}{-10} = 5$$

FIGURE 3-2   Assessing Mathematics Intuition

Answer the following without using a calculator or making pencil-and-paper calculations. Work as quickly as you can.

1. Which of the following are incorrect answers?

20 × 5 = 100	20 × 10 = 2000	20 × 50 = 2000
50 × 5 = 200	50 × 10 = 500	80 × 10 = 300
30 × 50 = 1000	30 × 5 = 150	15 × 3 = 35
150 × 3 = 350	15 × 30 = 350	25 × 5 = 125
150 ÷ 3 = 45	300 ÷ 20 = 15	450 ÷ 15 = 30
2000 ÷ 50 = 40	1000 ÷ 5 = 200	1500 ÷ 45 = 3
500 ÷ 20 = 30	10000 ÷ 10 = 100	300 ÷ 15 = 25

2. What single error do the following have in common?

136 × 2 = 262	75 × 5 = 350	14 + 14 + 16 = 34
1979 + 17 = 1986	25 × 25 = 505	15 × 15 × 5 = 255

3. What tells you at a glance that the following answers are wrong?

9750 − 47 = 9700	670 − 58 = 620	11780 − 10777 = 900
99 × 120 = 10979	620 × 720 = 386444	1940 × 1940 = 37636

$$\frac{5}{6} \div \frac{1}{6} = \frac{5}{36} \qquad \frac{1}{2} \div \frac{1}{2} = \frac{1}{4} \qquad \frac{3}{21} \div \frac{2}{3} = \frac{6}{63} \qquad \frac{4}{12} \div \frac{1}{3} = \frac{4}{36}$$

2.36 × 1.5 = 354	.56 × .99 = 55.44	4.325 × .001 = 43.2
1100 ÷ 3 = 370	$100 \times \frac{2}{7} = 30$	444 ÷ 5 = 86

4. Create shortcuts for doing the following problems:

99 + 98 + 97 + 95 + 94 + 93 + 92 + 91 + 90 =
99 × 99 × 99 × 99 × 99 × 99 =
120)‾15000   1000)‾76667000   10,000)‾10,000
10 − 7 + 10 − 2 + 10 − 5 + 10 − 8 + 10 − 3 + 10 − 9 =

5. Quick-guess approximate answers to the following:

102)‾5642 =	98 × 673 =	999 × 5672 =	99)‾1287
50)‾3999 =	48 × 48 =	24)‾125500 =	1102 × 733 =
798 × 802 =	12)‾14448 =	25)‾99892 =	4.9 × 2222 =

Student-Hostile Teaching Strategies

In Teaching Scenario #1 at the beginning of this chapter, we saw a classic example of anxiety-producing teaching. Unfortunately, the methods and the philosophy that inspires them are neither uncommon nor universally deplored. In a recent meeting, a math educator explained his philosophy of teaching in this way:

> Forget pedagogy. Forget math anxiety and other excuses to mollycoddle the students. We have the subject matter. We lecture on the subject matter. We test on the subject matter. If the students can't cut it, they don't belong in the class.

In my opinion, the one who does not belong in that class is the teacher. Taken to its logical conclusion, his argument would exclude a large portion of the population from receiving any type of math education. Sixty percent of the teacher trainees tested using the Math Anxiety Self Quiz (see Figure 2-1) claimed to be highly math anxious; 30 percent claimed to be moderately math anxious; and many attributed their anxiety to hostile teaching strategies. Some of the most frequently mentioned include the following:

1. Verbally abusing students for errors—being called math-dumb, bonehead, knucklehead, peabrain
2. Punishing behavior and deficiences with math exercises
3. Exposing students to public ridicule by assigning board problems or badgering the unprepared
4. Isolating the learners—"Keep your eyes on the board. There will be no talking, no exchanging of notes or papers and no questions for anyone but the teacher."
5. Ramrodding information—"Listen up. I'm going to say this one time and one time only."
6. Input/output teaching—Without interacting with students, teacher inputs information to them through lectures and study assignments; students output information to teacher by doing homework and taking tests.

Punishing students for errors, with words or behaviors, dehumanizes them and the learning process. It restricts learning by in effect short-circuiting the learning process. Instead of making errors as an integral part of learning, making errors in effect becomes the end of the process. Similarly, restrictive teaching strategies limit the opportunities for learning. They create what amounts to a learning tunnel, a narrow corridor along which information can flow; learning, then, from peers or experiences outside the tunnel is severely restricted.

Math-Hostile Teaching Strategies

Although the effects of math-hostile teaching strategies are less immediate and traumatic, they are nonetheless serious. The teachers in Scenarios #2 and #3 at the beginning of this chapter are in fact using student-friendly strategies, but at the same time their hostility toward the subject is fostering attitudes and deficiences that will impact their students' math learning for years to come.

Some of the symptoms of math-hostile teaching follow:

1. Verbally abusing the subject (rather than the students)
2. Avoiding the teaching of concepts—relegating math lessons to aides, student assistants, exercise books, or computers
3. Overemphasizing the spoonful-of-sugar technique—"Math is bad medicine, but a game or story or art project will help us stomach it."
4. Substituting pushbutton math for real math learning—that is, teaching the use of calculators or computers rather than the use of students' minds
5. Unconsciously sabotaging math studies—devoting less class time to math, giving less math homework, scheduling math lessons only before lunch or at the end of the day when attention spans are generally shorter
6. Apologizing for the subject—"I'm sorry, but we have to study our math lesson."
7. Making excuses for shortcomings in skill or commitment—"I'm a left-brained artist, not a mathematician."

Ultimately, math-hostile teaching impacts student behaviors as well as attitudes. A child influenced to avoid math in elementary school will probably avoid math electives in high school, will not become a math major in college, and will sidestep careers that require mathematical expertise.

Student-Friendly/Math-Friendly Teaching Strategies

Avoiding math-anxious teaching calls for teaching strategies that are both student friendly and math friendly. Successful math teaching employs, not a single teaching strategy, but a repertoire of strategies. Which strategy a teacher uses will depend on the lesson topic, the students' intellectual development and motivation, and available learning materials, as well as on the teacher's own math background and attitudes.

1. *Ausubel's advance organizers:* This teaching strategy, named for its originator, David Ausubel, is basically deductive—working from the general to the specific—but unlike the traditional lecture method, it approaches learning as an integrative process. The starting point and end point of the learning process are children's *knowledge schemes*—the patterns that organize and coordinate knowledge.

An existing knowledge scheme provides the foundation for introducing a new concept, relationship, or operation. Then an *advanced organizer* shows the new pattern to be tied to the scheme. The teacher begins the process of integration with examples and illustrations, and students complete it as they apply the new pattern in exercises or projects.

For example, to introduce multiplication, you would begin with the children's existing knowledge scheme for addition, then use "repeated addition" as an advance organizer for the lesson.

$$6 + 6 = 12 \qquad 4 + 4 + 4 + 4 = 16 \qquad 8 + 8 + 8 = 24$$
$$2 \times 6 = 12 \qquad\quad 4 \times 4 = 16 \qquad\qquad 3 \times 8 = 24$$

The advance organizer functions in the manner of a Gestalt insight: the concept, relationship, or pattern is grasped all at once, rather than piecemeal. The danger, of course, lies in students' memorizing a rule or principle by rote and applying it mechanically without meaningful learning. Teachers will avoid this trap if they first accurately assess students' existing knowledge schemes; second, design advance organizers to stretch those schemes without breaking them—that is, without abandoning all existing referents; and, third, provide ample practice and support for integration.

2. *Discovery learning:* Based on the work of Jerome Bruner, discovery learning involves inductive reasoning and Socratic teaching strategies. This is learning by the scientific method. Students interact with data in the form of examples, exercises, or activities with manipulatives. Teachers guide this interaction with carefully structured questions that lead the students step by step from understanding individual problems to inferring general patterns or principles or rules.

For example, in the following scenario the teacher leads the students to discover the procedure for dividing by fractions.

Scenario #4

Several fifth-graders are working at a large table. They have been using compasses to draw circles of various radii.

The teacher has been moving around the table, looking over shoulders and making suggestions. Now she calls for the students' attention and asks, "How many circles have you made?"

The students count quickly and answer, "Five."

"All right. Now take a ruler and draw a line through the center of each circle."

The students draw the lines.

The teacher is ready with her next question, "When you draw a line through the middle of a circle, what do you get?"

"A half."

"Just one half?"

"No, two halves for each circle."

"How many halves for the five circles?"

"Two, four, six, eight, ten!"

The teacher moves now to the chalkboard. "How would we write that in words?"

"Five circles divided in half make ten halves."

The teacher writes, then asks,"How would we write that in numbers? Try it on your own paper."

The students scribble for a minute, look at each other's papers, then write some more.

Finally, one student speaks up, "We didn't all do it the same way."

"That's fine, let's look at all the ways."

After several minutes of discussion, the chalkboard shows three different ways to write the problem in numbers:

$$\frac{5}{\frac{1}{2}} = 10, \qquad \frac{1}{2}\overline{\smash{\big)}5} = 10, \qquad 5 \div \frac{1}{2} = 10$$

Once the students have repeated the process with quarters, eighths, and sixteenths, the teacher calls their attention to the chalkboard, now covered with numbers.

"Whenever we divide a fraction, what happens? Do we end up with more than we started with or less?"

"More!"

"How much more?"

More scribbling. A minute passes.

"As much as if we multiply by the fraction."

The teacher writes quickly on the chalkboard:

$$5 \times \frac{1}{2} = \frac{5}{2}$$

"Is this what you mean?"

"No, turn the fraction over. Then multiply."

$$\frac{5}{1} \div \frac{1}{2} = \frac{5}{1} \times \frac{2}{1} = 10$$

The students in this scenario have "discovered" the pattern underlying a standard math procedure, then inferred the procedure from the pattern. The teacher has guided the process by asking the right questions—something that requires not only hearing what the students are saying but also intuiting what they are thinking.

The special advantage of discovery learning is thoroughness; one disadvantage is slowness. Moreover, because there is no guarantee that all members of a study group have actually "discovered" a knowledge structure, the question–answer process may have to be repeated individually or reinforced with Ausubel-style organizers and integration activities.

3. *Conditioning:* Whether conditioning is a hostile or a friendly strategy depends primarily on how it is used. As we have seen, the affective components of math anxiety are often conditioned—negative associations that become entangled with math learning until they impede or even halt progress.

But conditioning can also work the other way. I know one teacher who plays Mozart recordings during math lessons so that students will associate math with the order and elegance of classical music. Another teaches math outside on sunny days.

As a teaching tool, conditioning relies on both association and repetition. Therefore, if we want students to associate math with positive things—good feelings, good music, good times—we can build those associations into our lesson plans. If we want the associations to become a permanent part of the students' learning, we must repeat them over and over and over again.

What about memorizing? Rote memorization has, of course, been a whipping post for progressive educators; however, memorizing need not be by rote. Students who understand that multiplication is repeated addition and have integrated the process into their own knowledge schemes might memorize the times tables as a shortcut. They know how to perform the underlying operation; they can cross-check their answers if necessary. But the constant and repeated need for the information throughout basic arithmetic operations makes the shortcut of memorizing worthwhile.

I have often made memorizing part of a human-calculator game. Input the numbers by memorizing in a systematic pattern—$2 \times 2 = 4$, $2 \times 3 = 6$, $2 \times 4 = 8$, and so forth. Then output with problems selected at random—$6 \times 8 = 48$, $12 \times 3 = 36$, $7 \times 7 = 49$, and so forth. As part of the game, I match human calculator against electronic calculator. Usually, for two-digit problems at least, the human calculator will win.

4. *Positive reinforcement:* Although this is sometimes called the "reward system," positive reinforcement involves more than supplying rewards for students' accomplishments. Another form of conditioning, it works on the principle that learning is a response shaped by consequences. An event, called a discriminative stimulus, initiates the process, leading to a response and a consequence. If the response is positive, a positive consequence will strengthen and perpetuate it.

You will notice that I am not adding what may appear to be a logical corollary: If the response is negative, a negative consequence (like punishment) will necessarily weaken and eventually halt it. Positive reinforcement does not, and will not work as half of a carrots-and-stick strategy: carrots for rewards, the stick for punishment. While positive consequences promote positive learning cycles, punishment does not work in reverse. In fact, while punishment may discourage the immediate display of behavior, it causes the behavior to be suppressed rather than eliminated. Moreover, it actively promotes anxiety-related responses, including negative emotions such as hostility and fear and negative learning patterns such as avoidance.

So what do we do if we cannot punish negative responses? We withhold rewards—not permanently but until we get the response we want. Mastery learning, which we will discuss in Chapter 10, works on this principle. The students continue studying a concept or procedure, such as multiplying decimals, and taking different forms of the mastery tests until they achieve mastery (often measured as an 80–90 percent test score). Mastery is rewarded, but failed attempts are not punished; therefore, the motivation is always forward—to keep studying, to keep trying, to keep reaching for the carrot.

While some teachers and parents use external rewards as reinforcers (money, treats, extra privileges, etc.), I prefer reinforcers—such as credit toward a grade, praise, or even stars and smiling faces—that can be tied more directly to the work itself. Children quickly develop an appetite for success; the more praise and good grades they receive, the more they want.

5. *Modeling:* All teachers are learning models. We model attitudes about learning, approaches to problem solving, ways to learn and ways not to learn. Moreover, while students may remember what we *tell* them, they are much more likely to remember what we *show* them.

As a teaching strategy, modeling incorporates some key principles of Albert Bandura's social learning theory. First, it involves observation learning. Most of the other strategies discussed here involve learning-by-doing, but modeling depends on learning-by-seeing. Second, it incorporates the effect on learning of variables like the complexity of the modeled behavior, the motivation to imitate the model, and the conditions for displaying or suppressing the behavior. The teacher in the first classroom scenario at the beginning of this chapter is acting out what I call the "show-off" model of problem solving. By keeping his explanation abstract and his demonstration brief, he makes the process appear too complex for students to imitate. The teachers in the second and third scenarios are more positive role models (their students probably want to be like them), but they are modeling negative attitudes about learning math.

Since modeling impacts both the affective and the cognitive domains of learning, teachers who are themselves math anxious may need in effect to write a script and play the role. Some *do's* and *don't's* for the role model math learner are listed in the chart in Figure 3-3.

Succeeding chapters will explore additional student-friendly/math-friendly teaching strategies, including instructional systems such as mastery learning. Creating a repertoire of strategies begins with assembling current techniques, review-

FIGURE 3-3   Modeling Math Learning

DO's	*DON'T'S*
1. DO model behaviors within students' capabilities to imitate.	1. DON'T model behaviors so complex that students cannot imitate them.
2. DO display behaviors you want students to learn.	2. DON'T display behaviors you do not want students to learn, excusing them with "do as I say, not as I do."
3. DO model problem-solving strategies—approaches that work.	3. DON'T use negative models—approaches that do not work.
4. DO remember that learning may be latent—undisplayed for years.	4. DON'T assume that lack of display equals lack of learning.
5. DO plan lessons holistically, coordinating audio, visual, and tactile experiences.	5. DON'T focus on what you say to the students to the exclusion of what you show them and what they do.

ing your own math attitudes and competence, and understanding your students' developmental levels and needs. If you are math anxious about fractions but fractions are part of your class curriculum, you may need to start by increasing your own proficiency, then select strategies for teaching that allow you maximum preparation for the modeling role. If you are confident but your students are anxious, you might adopt a strategy such as discovery learning that allows them to move at their own pace and feel their way. Whether you yourself are math anxious or math confident, Activity #2 in the end-of-chapter exercises gives you the opportunity to develop both a purpose and a plan for avoiding math-anxious teaching.

Questions for Thought and Discussion

1. Have you experienced math-anxious teaching strategies? What were they, and what were their effects on your math learning?

2. Have you ever used math-anxious teaching strategies? What were they, and what were their effects on your students?

3. How confident are you about your own math skills? Would you describe your math proficiency as student-level or teacher-level?

4. What student-friendly/math-friendly strategies could you add to the list begun in this chapter? What makes those strategies student friendly? What makes them math friendly?

Activities

1. Write your own teaching scenarios for a lesson that you believe would build math confidence and a lesson that would contribute to math anxiety.
2. Prepare a profile of your own math teaching. Assess your strengths and weaknesses. Then establish goals for overcoming the weaknesses and building on the strengths, and prepare a semester (or term) plan for meeting those goals.

Annotated List of Readings

Ausubel, David. P., V. D. Novak, and H. Hanesian. *Educational Psychology: A Cognitive View,* 2nd ed. New York: Holt, Rinehart and Winston, 1978. *Seminal work on Ausubel's expository teaching. Provides a theoretical foundation and concrete examples applicable to the classroom.*

Biehler, Robert. F., and Jack Snowman. *Psychology Applied to Teaching,* 7th ed. Boston: Houghton Mifflin, 1993. *Readable overview of approaches to learning and applications to classroom situations.*

Bruner, Jerome S. *Toward a Theory of Instruction.* New York: Norton, 1966. *Foundation for current discovery learning techniques.*

Skinner, B. F. *The Technology of Teaching.* Englewood Cliffs, NJ: Prentice-Hall, 1968. *Classic treatment of operant conditioning applications to classroom concerns.*

4

Diagnosing and
Treating the
Math-Anxious Student

What if a child is already math anxious? Although prevention always works better than therapy, no one teacher can control all the factors impacting students' math learning. A math-anxious parent, a teacher who avoids numbers, a teacher who does not explain math-related ideas, an embarrassing experience associated with learning math, a failed attempt at learning math—any of these factors can provide the impetus for math anxiety or keep a cycle of math anxiety going.

Generally, the less math instruction children have had, the less math anxiety they exhibit. Therefore, children in kindergarten or the early grades are less likely to be math anxious than children in the later grades. Does this mean that mathematics as a discipline generates anxiety? Not at all. But it does make many methods of math instruction suspect, as well as the behaviors of many math instructors.

Diagnosis

Many adults are quick to tell me, "I'm math anxious. I've been afraid of math since grade school." Children, however, rarely label their negative feelings as math anxiety. They will say, "I hate math. It's boring. Subtraction is dumb. I can't do fractions. My teacher is stupid. Who needs math?" Sometimes, like Calvin, they will either refuse to try or will sabotage their own efforts by diverting their attention from the problem at hand.

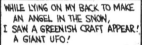

FIGURE 4-1 Math Behaviors Worksheet

Student's Name _____ Philip Vigil _____

Behaviors	Mon.	Tue.	Wed.	Thurs.	Fri.	Comments
			Weekday Occurrences			
1. Does not do homework.	X	X	X	X	X	Did not take work home.
2. Does poorly on test or exercise.	X	X		X	X	Skipped most problems on test.
3. Does not do classwork.	X	X			X	
4. Does not pay attention.	X			X	X	Throws spitballs at girls, spends most of the period looking out of window. Makes paper cutouts.
5. Makes negative comments about math.	X	X		X	X	Said, "Fractions are stupid," and "Nobody uses fractions."
6. Refuses to answer questions about math.	X		X		X	Shrugs rather than answers.
7. Displays negative body language.	X	X	X	X	X	Frowns, slouches, lays head on hands and arms frequently.
8. Makes excuses to avoid math.	X	X		X	X	Asks to go to restroom, water fountain, or time-out room often.
9. Appears agitated or uncomfortable during math exercises.	X		X	X	X	
10. Displays or displaces frustration—tears book pages or exercises, etc.	X					Crumples worksheet and throws it on the floor.
11. Other negative behaviors imitated from classmates.	X			X	X	Drooling on math exercises; laughing at other students who give correct answers.

43

Identifying a Problem

To diagnose adult math anxiety, we used primarily a metacognitive approach—that is, techniques that prompted the adults to think about their thinking as well as their feelings. To diagnosis children's math anxiety, we begin by observing behaviors. Does the child do poorly in math? Are homework assignments avoided? Are there frequent trips to the water fountain or the restroom during math instruction? Does the child get sick during quizzes or tests in math? Does attention wander during math lessons? Does body language signal distaste, boredom, or anger during math instruction? The Math Behavior Worksheet, Figure 4-1 on page 43, shows how one teacher tracked a student's behaviors through a school week.

Philip's math behaviors are primarily negative, but they do show a pattern. Although he generally avoids math—skipping homework assignments, not paying attention in class, refusing to work problems or answer questions— the negative behaviors are most apparent before and immediately after the weekend, which he spends at home with his father. Moreover, Philip quotes his father as saying, "Nobody uses fractions." The pattern, then, revealed by the worksheet, not only shows a math-anxiety construct with interacting affective and cognitive factors, but also points toward the child's home as a possible source of the problem.

The Math Attitude Quizzes on pages 44–45 can also red-flag anxiety problems. While teachers may assign the quizzes to older children as a pencil-and-paper exercise, they should give the quiz to younger children orally, either in one-to-one conferences or in small groups. Generally, if there are more *no* than *yes* responses, the child may be math anxious, and the greater number of *no* responses, the greater the anxiety.

Notice that, even though we discussed anxiety openly in diagnosing math-anxious adults, with children we use neutral terms like *attitude*. This helps us avoid the anxiety-by-suggestion trap. For an adult, admitting math anxiety is the first step toward taking control and overcoming it; for a child, who is not yet equipped to be in control, placing a label on vague fears and behaviors tends to substantiate and even legitimize them.

Because it is normal for children to enjoy learning and feel confident about their abilities, statements about likes and dislikes can be revealing, particularly for the younger children. Moreover, since children often project their own feelings on others, their interpretations of teachers', parents', and friends' likes and dislikes may reflect both external influences and personal attitude.

Math Attitude Quiz #1 (Oral for Grades 1–2)

Read the following questions aloud. Mark student answers on individual sheets.

	Yes	No
1. Do you like numbers?	___	___
2. Do you like arithmetic?	___	___
3. Do you always do your math homework?	___	___
4. Are you good at math?	___	___

5. Is counting easy?   ____ ____
6. Does your teacher like math?   ____ ____
7. Does your Mom like math?   ____ ____
8. Does your Dad like math?   ____ ____
9. Is it important to learn math?   ____ ____
10. Have you learned to add?   ____ ____
11. Have you learned to subtract?   ____ ____
12. Can you learn to multiply and divide?   ____ ____

Math Attitude Quiz #2 (Oral or Written, Grades 3–4)

Answer each of the following questions. Put an X in the *yes* or *no* column.

		Yes	*No*
1.	Do you like numbers?	____	____
2.	Do you like math class?	____	____
3.	Are you good at math?	____	____
4.	Do you always do your math homework?	____	____
5.	Do you always pay attention during math?	____	____
6.	Is it important to learn math?	____	____
7.	Have you learned to multiply?	____	____
8.	Have you learned to divide?	____	____
9.	Can you learn fractions?	____	____
10.	Can you learn decimals?	____	____
11.	Do your friends like math?	____	____
12.	Does your teacher like math?	____	____

Math Attitude Quiz #3 (Written, Grades 5–6)

Answer each of the following questions by marking an X in the *yes* or *no* column. Work quickly, putting down the first response that comes to mind.

		Yes	*No*
1.	Do you like working with numbers?	____	____
2.	Do you like doing your math homework?	____	____
3.	Are you good at math?	____	____
4.	Is it important to learn math?	____	____
5.	Can you solve most of the math problems in your assignments?	____	____
6.	Can you understand most of the concepts in your math lessons?	____	____
7.	Are you looking forward to learning algebra?	____	____
8.	Are you usually praised for your work in math?	____	____
9.	Does solving math problems make you feel good?	____	____
10.	Are you comfortable with word problems?	____	____

Understanding a Problem

Once a problem has been identified, the next step is to define it—to discover its parameters, to assess its intensity, to uncover causes and trace effects. Three helpful tools in the defining process are the problem-solving protocol, the math history, and cognitive-affective measures such as the Math Problems and Mini-Math Anxiety Scale from Chapter 2.

1. *Problem-solving protocol:* The protocol is a record of a child's thoughts and reactions during the problem-solving process. The child is given a series of problems, beginning with ones he or she can solve easily, then becoming progressively more difficult and including one or more problems the child probably cannot solve. As the child works, a monitor asks questions and makes a record of the process, either in writing or on a tape. A transcript of a protocol might begin something like this:

Monitor: How would you read this first problem?
Student: Twelve times eleven. That means you multiply.
Monitor: How would you do that?
Student: Well first you go one times twelve. Then you move over one space and go, one times twelve.
Monitor: Then what?
Student: Then you add. The two comes down. Two plus one is three, and the one comes down. So you get one hundred and thirty two.
Monitor: Are you sure that's right?
Student: Yes. I dunno. I guess so.
Monitor: Can you show me by dividing?
Student: Dividing's harder.
Monitor: Why?
Student: I hate dividing.

2. *The math history:* Older children can record their own math histories, beginning with when they learned to count and tell time. Because the purpose here is to elicit as much detail as possible, I find it helpful to guide the activity either with oral questions or with a worksheet. For a chronological history, the initial questions emphasize *when:* When did you learn to count? To tell time? To add? To subtract? Then, to identify key events, the questions emphasize *what:* What happened when you were learning to count? And to discover important influences, the questions emphasize *who:* Who taught you to count, add, subtract, and so forth?

Children's math histories may or may not be accurate. They may even include contradictory information—for example, the child who recalls both liking and disliking his first arithmetic lessons. But, whether accurate or inaccurate, the histories offer insights on the way the children perceive their own math learning and some important clues to what works or does not work for them.

3. *Cognitive-affective measures:* Instruments like the Math Problems and Mini-Math Anxiety Scale in Figure 2-2 can be tailored to fit your students. Begin by selecting problems that match their current skills levels; add some that stretch their skills, then pair the problems with an attitude assessment scale. Again, the instrument can be administered orally to younger children and as a paper-and-pencil exercise to older children.

As with adults, the cognitive-affective measure helps identify specific skills gaps and trace some of the interactions between negative performance and negative emotions. With fourth-graders and above, I particularly like to include some word problems, and at least one of those problems will be a word version of an earlier numbers problem. Generally, anxiety levels increase and performance declines on word problems—probably because they call for math reasoning rather than simply following procedures mapped out by symbols such as plus or minus or division signs. Figure 4-2 shows the first page of a test designed for sixth-graders.

FIGURE 4-2   Math Problems (Grade 6)

Show all work on this sheet or on extra sheets.

1. $1/4 + 1/2 - 6/8 =$
2. $1/5 \times 2/3 - 3/8 =$
3. $15/16 - 12/8 =$
4. $7/9 - 4/5 + 3/11 =$
5. $.32 \times .28 =$
6. $.51 \times .37 =$
7. $.12 - .13 + .01 =$
8. $.001 - .01 + .10 =$
9. $.01 \times .02 =$
10. $.17 \times .18 =$

Change the following decimals to percentages.

11. $.01$
12. $.333$
13. 4.1
14. $.001$
15. 1.001
16. 3.12

Change the following percentages into decimals.

17. 5%
18. 100%
19. 16%
20. 1.2%
21. $.05\%$
22. $.003\%$

Solving the following word problems.

23. What percentage of 100 is 18?
24. What percentage of 10 is 6?
25. What percentage of 120 is 20?
26. What percentage of 180 is 32?

Developing a Math Learning Profile

After we have collected data about a child's skills, attitudes, and math background, we are ready to develop a Math Learning Profile (Figure 4-3). An overall picture of a learning history, a profile maps information in a way that highlights patterns and facilitates interpreting relationships. For example, the profile for Philip Vigil, the subject of the Math Observation Worksheet at the beginning of this chapter, was compiled not only from his teacher's observations and records but also from a written math history and a cognitive-affective test.

FIGURE 4-3   Math Learning Profile

For Philip Vigil, Age 11

	Strengths	*Weaknesses*
Skills	addition/multiplication/ decimals/word problems with money/ working with computers and calculators/	subtraction (multiple digits)/ division/fractions/ word problems involving physical relationships/ working with manipulatives/
Attitudes	likes finance, enjoys problems involving money/	says math is boring, useless/ becomes agitated during tests/ feels hostile toward teacher/hates fractions/no confidence in answers, whether right or wrong/
Behaviors	attends school most days/ helps other students when problems involve finance/ will do exercises on classroom computer/	does not do math homework/ cheats on tests/does not pay attention/abuses math material/ disrupts math class/makes excuses to leave class/refuses to answer questions/will not do paper-and-pencil exercises
Background	could count to 100 before kindergarten/learned to make change before 6/ won a class adding-bee in 2nd grade/quantitative scores on IQ test—above average	his father dislikes math/ punishment for errors in 2nd and 3rd grades/ missed several weeks of school in 4th grade because of illness/average grades in math until 4th grade, then most unsatisfactory/quantitative scores on achievement test—below average

First, Philip's profile confirms what we suspected from the earlier observations: Philip dislikes what he has trouble doing, he is not receiving support at home, and his disruptive behavior is tied specifically to problems with math learning. Second, the profile helps us place Philip's current behavior in context. He did not always hate math, and he still does not hate all math. He likes what he does well at and is interested in and even enjoys demonstrating his competence to classmates. Moreover, Philip's performance does not accurately reflect his abilities: he should be doing average to above-average work. Third, the profile points toward some possible causes, including some gaps in knowledge, a possible lag in his developing the reasoning skills for reversibility (needed for subtraction and division), negative experiences tied to learning attempts, and negative attitudes acquired at home. Finally, the profile suggests an opening for treatment. Because Philip does like finance and works well with computers and calculators, his teacher can approach his knowledge and skills gaps through computer exercises about money. And, because he likes to display his knowledge by helping other students, the teacher can build his confidence through teacher-aide assignments.

Because they can recognize symptoms from experience, math-anxious or recovering math-anxious teachers often excel at diagnosing math anxiety among their students. Teachers who are not math anxious will need to train themselves to watch for warning signs: changes in classroom behavior or performance, hostility, hyperactivity or inactivity during lessons, approach–avoidance behaviors, short attention spans.

Treatment

Because of its complexity, math anxiety resists the quick fix. No one becomes math anxious overnight, and no one recovers math confidence after a day or two of intervention. I once worked with an eight-year-old whose father had been a math major in college. The boy could count and add small numbers, but he could not subtract well and he would not tackle multiplication. "I think he's learning disabled," the father told me. Over a period of several weeks, we traced at least some of the problem to slow development of reasoning skills paired with the father's early carrots-and-stick attempts to accelerate the boy's math learning. Oddly, we eventually discovered that the father himself had developed slowly and had been tutored and drilled relentlessly in basic math skills by his older sisters, who were teachers. He later admitted to me that, although he was a good mathematician, he did not really like numbers.

Although preventing math anxiety can be a group project, treatment must be individual. To be effective, a treatment program must both alleviate the symptoms and strike at the causes of those symptoms, and it must also break the cycle of behaviors that perpetuates the problem.

Making a Treatment Plan

Which techniques fit which problems and which students depends on age, current skills development, and experience as well as the degree of anxiety. However, whatever the specific situation, some general principles apply:

• If there are gaps in learning, they must be filled in.
• If there are bad learning habits, they must be replaced by good learning habits.
• If there is a history of math failures, it must be countered with a history of math successes.
• If there are negative attitudes, they must be replaced by positive attitudes.

Most treatment will begin with an Individualized Study Plan (ISP) and rely heavily on one-to-one instruction. The purpose of the plan, of course, is to fill in gaps; however, the work should begin, not at the gap, but before it. For example, for a student who multiplies well but has problems with decimals, the ISP would start with multiplication; for a student who can add well but not subtract, the ISP would start with addition. In this way, the student builds confidence and accesses functional learning pathways rather than those made dysfunctional by distress.

Motivating a math-anxious student to concentrate on math requires patience and perseverance. Often progress will come by inches rather than feet—something that can be just as discouraging to the teacher as to the student. Initially, you may need to reinforce attempts as well as actual successes—completing part of an assignment, getting one answer correct, executing part of a procedure successfully. Figure 4-4 on page 51 shows how reinforcement can be used to condition increasingly complex behaviors.

To lead the student from point A, not doing math homework, to point B, doing the work correctly and handing it in on time, the teacher devises a conditioning chain. First, she focuses on doing the work and reinforces each progressive step toward the goal of doing all the work. Then she piggybacks a second goal, getting the work in on time, and reinforces responses that maintain the first goal and make progress toward the second. Finally, she adds the third goal, doing the work correctly, and reinforces responses that maintain the first two goals and make progress toward the third. When progress breaks down at any point in the chain, she simply withholds reinforcement until the response gets back on track.

The effectiveness of the conditioning chain depends partly on the scheduling and partly on the motivational value of the reinforcers. I believe, as I said earlier, that the best reinforcers are those tied most closely to the learning task. Ultimately,

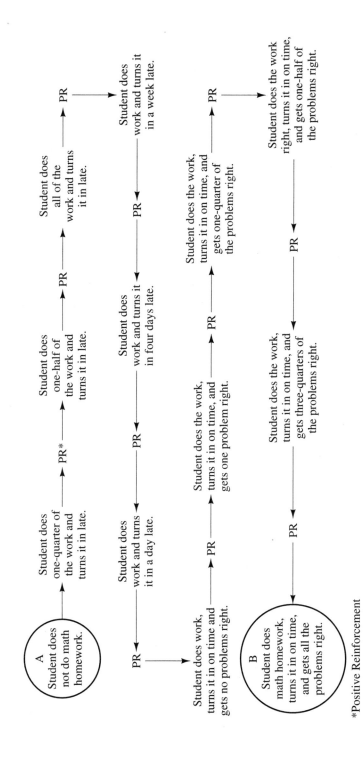

*Positive Reinforcement

FIGURE 4-4   Math Homework Conditioning Chain

we want to foster a system of internal reinforcement in which doing a job well is rewarded by feelings of accomplishment, satisfaction, and well-being. Nonetheless, motivating a child who, for the moment at least, does not like math to study math diligently may require some external rewards. One teacher uses play money, which can be spent on toys or school items during the class's weekly store day. Another uses food treats—her version, she says, of Pavlov-style training. Others work with parents who offer money, privileges, outings (to the zoo, a theme park, a sports event, and so forth), or some item the child wants badly enough to work for it. Although some educators feel that these types of reinforcers set bad precedents—like bribing a child to behave—I see them as a temporary drastic measure, akin to the rocket booster on a space flight: its quick burst of energy is necessary to get the craft moving, but once escape velocity has been achieved, it can be quickly jettisoned and forgotten.

Spacing reinforcement is easy at the beginning of treatment: simply reinforce each behavior that meets or brings the student closer to the goals. Once the goals are reached, however, maintaining the behavior may call for a different approach. Too often, treatment follows a roller-coaster path—uphill as a child is drawn along a conditioning chain, then downhill as the ground gained is lost and previous behavior patterns reassert themselves. To establish a new, positive behavior pattern, it must be maintained over an extended period. This means changing the schedule of reinforcement. Oddly, what works best to maintain a behavior is not a regular schedule—rewards at either a set frequency or a set interval—but an irregular schedule—rewards set at either variable frequencies or variable intervals. The one-armed bandit schedule is an example of a variable frequency reinforcement schedule because it works in the same way as a Las Vegas slot machine: just when the player is ready to quit, the machine pays off. With either gambling or learning, the schedule conditions persistent and consistent effort because the players or learners believe there will be a payoff if they just keep at it. On the other hand, a regular schedule seems to foster cyclic effort, with bursts of activity right before a reward is due followed by a lull in actvity after the reward. A fixed interval schedule of reinforcement is notorious for resulting in such behavior cycles.

Although conditioning can help break a negative learning pattern and ample doses of math instruction will begin to fill in gaps, we must still deal with the symptoms of math anxiety. Some remedies that I have observed or have used successfully are listed in the chart in Figure 4-5 (page 53). No one technique works for every child, and some techniques work for only a limited time. Changing techniques periodically improves effectiveness and avoids the Not-that-again! response. Although the remedies do not really strike at the causes of math anxiety, they can alleviate the symptoms enough to give the individual treatment plan a chance to work.

FIGURE 4-5   Symptoms and Remedies

Math-Anxiety Symptoms	*Remedial Techniques*
Emotional distress during math activities	1. The spoonful of sugar: teaching with stories, games, or jokes; combining study with treats or privileges 2. Mary Poppins in the classroom: role playing, performing, clowning 3. Music and aroma therapy
Physical distress during math activities	1. Physical exercise before, during, and after study 2. Lessons held outside on grass or among trees 3. Laughing, smiling exercises: Who can laugh the loudest? Who can smile the biggest? Who can grin the widest?
Hostility/anger	1. Write-it-out exercises: "I hate math because . . ." 2. Venting activities such as beating on a punching bag or a Bobo doll, growling, scowling
Lack of attention	1. Shock treatment: wearing a clown nose and wig during lessons, staging slapstick demonstrations 2. Participation activities: singing or chanting multiplication tables, talking out problems, round-robin problem solving (first student does first step, second student second step, etc.)
Fear of numbers	1. Desensitizing activities—numbers linked to relaxing and pleasant activities or things, songs about numbers, food with numbers (such as cupcakes, sweets, or popcorn, etc.), pleasant pictures associated with numbers, a cutout numbers zoo

Questions for Thought and Discussion

1. How might a child's math anxiety differ from an adult's?
2. How might adults be involved in a child's math anxiety?
3. Why is curing math anxiety more difficult than preventing it?
4. What role can math-confident children play in treating math-anxious children?

Activities

1. Develop math learning profiles for one or more elementary-level children. What do the profiles tell you about the children's current learning behaviors? What do they suggest about future needs or potential?
2. Develop a cognitive-affective instrument for measuring math skills and attitudes at the third-grade level.
3. Prepare a treatment plan for the following math-anxious students (or you may substitute students from your own classes or experiences).
   a. Mary is nine years old, and she thinks math is a boys' subject. She can add and multiply if she has to, but subtraction and division are difficult for her. She rarely completes her math assignments. She works just hard enough to get a passing grade on tests.
   b. Tino is eleven years old. He has always liked math and wants to be a computer scientist someday. But he is having problems with fractions and is beginning to develop a bad attitude. He has told his classmates that studying fractions is dumb, and his parents say that his teacher can't teach fractions.

Annotated List of Readings

Tobias, Sheila. *Overcoming Math Anxiety.* Boston: Houghton Mifflin, 1978. *Classic early work on the causes, effects, and treatment of math anxiety. Deals with math anxiety in general and also in relation to specific topics such as gender and word problems.*

Arem, Cynthia. *Conquering Math Anxiety: A Self-Help Workbook.* Pacific Grove, CA: Brooks/Cole, 1993. *A practical hands-on approach to treating math anxiety. Presents tips and exercises that can be adapted for various ages.*

5

Creating an Anxiety-
Free Math Class

Recently I asked several student teachers to describe an anxiety-free math class. Their responses highlight a central dilemma of math teaching: How do you teach a subject that many students find difficult without creating some anxiety?

"An anxiety-free class is one where the children are relaxed and enjoying their work."
"An anxiety-free class is a happy class."
"In an anxiety-free class no one is learning much math. There has to be some anxiety to get the job done."

Are learning and enjoyment mutually exclusive? No. Must children be anxious to work hard? No. At the same time a too-relaxed attitude might very well mean that "no one is learning much math," for an anxiety-free class is not the same thing as a stress-free class.

Stress, of course, is not a popular word. Being "under" stress evokes images of Atlas shouldering the world, Alka-Seltzer cocktails, Maalox moments. But stress is an essential ingredient of living. Hans Selye, whose work forms the core of modern stress research, often commented, "When you stop feeling stress, you're dead." Predictably, there is good stress and there is bad stress. Selye called them *eustress* and *distress.* As with good and bad cholesterol, we need eustress to live, to learn, to meet challenges and make progress toward goals; distress threatens our quality of life and our learning and impedes our progress.

Because math anxiety is essentially distress associated with math learning, we can eliminate it without sacrificing the qualities that encourage excellence. Recall the methods of Jaime Escalante, the East Los Angeles math teacher whose work

Confidence Level

	Confident	Not Confident
Knowing	Eustress	Distress/Eustress
Not Knowing	Eustress/Distress	Distress

(row label at left: Knowledge)

FIGURE 5-1   Eustress/Distress Relationships between Knowledge and Confidence Level

was the subject of the movie *Stand and Deliver.* Escalante's classes were neither stress-free nor relaxing. He pushed and prodded his students to excel, but for the most part the stress in his classroom was eustress rather than distress.

The matrix in Figure 5-1 above shows how cognitive and affective factors interact to promote eustress and distress.

Pose a problem to a student who knows how to solve it and is confident in that knowledge, and the result will still be stress, but it will be eustress—the kind of emotional/mental surge that comes when people meet a challenge or rise to an occasion. Pose a problem to a student who does not know how to solve it and feels no confidence in the little knowledge that he or she has, and the result will be distress—a debilitating feeling that causes people to do less than their best, to sink beneath the problem. Moreover, pose problems to students who know the material but lack confidence or who feel confident but lack knowledge and the result will be a conflicting mixture of eustress and distress—"I can do math, but I hate it." "I liked numbers until I became math dumb in the fifth grade." "I never do math until I have to, but my grades are OK."

Maximizing conditions that promote knowledge and confidence, minimizing conditions that promote lack of knowledge and lack of confidence—these are essential ingredients for an anxiety-free math class. These conditions involve not only teaching methods (like those discussed in Chapter 4), but also student–teacher relationships, student–student relationships, instructional materials and systems, and even the learning environment of the class.

Creating a Learning-Friendly Environment

What makes a straight-rows, eyes-forward, look-at-the-chalkboard classroom so unfriendly to learning? To begin with, the arrangement fosters what I call ripple-effect learning. The teacher at the front of the room throws out an idea. It drops like a rock in a pond, creating waves that ripple throughout the room but decrease in force with distance and time. It also fosters a one-dimensional, photocopier-style learning process: The teacher inputs information; students output the same information, with the most exact copy receiving the highest grade.

But seating students in circles and small groups, changing the teacher's role from knowledge purveyor to learning facilitator, enlivening the atmosphere with color and plants, replacing chalkboards with overhead projectors or books with computers—none of these guarantees a learning-friendly environment. I have observed traditional classrooms where students actively learn, and I have observed innovative classrooms where students passively avoid learning. What makes the difference is not so much the physical arrangement as the classroom dynamics.

Figures 5-2 and 5-3 show the contrast between a math class with static dynamics and a math class with active dynamics. The x's in the diagram show the number of each student's responses (questions, answers, or comments), and the arrows show the direction of the responses (student to student or student to teacher). Notice that the physical arrangement of the classes is essentially the same. Both classes have adopted the less threatening circular seating with the teacher as part of the circle. Nonetheless, Figure 5-2 (below) shows a classroom dynamics that we usually associate with the straight-rows arrangement: responses are limited, and most are directed toward the teacher. The class dynamics diagrammed in Figure 5-3 on page 58 are both active and interactive: all of the students respond, and as many responses are directed to other students as to the teacher.

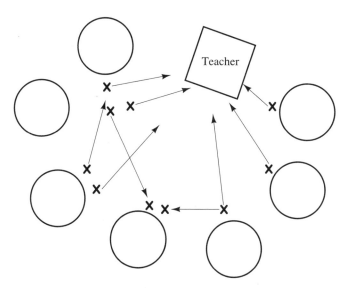

FIGURE 5-2   Static Dynamics

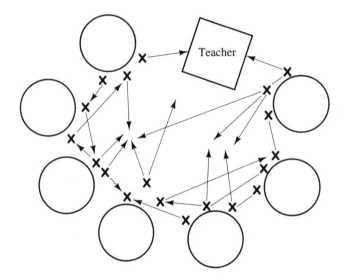

FIGURE 5-3   Active Dynamics

Some *do's* and *don't's* for promoting an active classroom dynamics follow:

Do's:

1. Encourage talking during math lessons if the talking is about math.
2. Encourage students to direct questions and answers to each other as well as to the teacher.
3. Reinforce comments, correct or incorrect, by treating all comments as important and by finding something positive to say about the mental processes that induced them, whatever their accuracy.
4. Manage class discussion so that all students are included, so that no students dominate and none are left out.
5. Learn to read body language so that you know when students want to be called on and when they do not, and respect their wishes.

Don't's:

1. Avoid take-turns activities—problem 1 for the first student, problem 2 for the second student, and so on around the room.
2. Resist the temptation to put unprepared students on the spot (spotlighting unpreparedness could be the math teacher's version of a public flogging).
3. Resist the temptation to demand the full attention of the class at all times and to be the class oracle—the only one to initiate discussion and answer questions.

4. Never put down students for incorrect answers—either directly with words or indirectly with body language; that short-circuits participation and discourages them from trying again.

5. Don't be afraid of productive noise or purposeful chaos. Active learning is rarely quiet, and it seldom operates effectively on the pushbutton, turn-it-on/turn-it-off principle.

Developing Learning-Friendly Classroom Management Systems

Closely related to classroom dynamics are access to knowledge and systems for feedback and evaluation. When students have immediate access to knowledge, question–answer activity increases and, with it, the volume of learning. When students receive immediate feedback, the pace of learning increases. And when evaluation provides impetus for the learning process rather than a conclusion to it, the motivation for learning increases.

1. *Increasing access to knowledge:* What happens when students have questions? Must they wait their turn to ask the teacher, or can they actively pursue the answers themselves? Centralizing sources of knowledge and prescribing specific patterns of inquiry—such as asking a teacher or aide—limit access to knowledge and restrict its pursuit. Broadening access begins with decentralizing and expanding resources and involves teaching the process of finding information as well as the information itself.

Teachers whose classrooms have multiple computer stations automatically decentralize the question–answer process. Most math learning programs encourage asking the computer rather than asking the teacher. However, classrooms with limited computer access can also decentralize with look-it-up stations such as a Mini–Math Library or Math Answers Boxes. Because students rarely ask new questions, most teachers can recite the important ones from memory. Write out those questions, the answers, and several examples; then file them in a tabbed box under headings such as Questions about Decimals, Questions about Multiplication, and so forth. The result is an easy-to-use resource that can be duplicated quickly and inexpensively with a photocopier.

Teaching students to answer their own questions means teaching them first to ask good questions and to ask often. A colleague who teaches calculus once told a class, "There are too many of you in this class; but I'm a good teacher; we have a good textbook; you won't need to ask any questions this semester." My colleague, of course, was attempting to reassure students intimidated by the size of the class and by the lack of personal attention; however, he was also suggesting a passive, spongelike role for his students. All they had to do was sit there and soak up calculus. Predictably, half of that class had either dropped out or flunked out by the end of the semester.

Some learning may take place in the passive, sponge mode, but it will be primarily rote memorized, conditioned responses without meaning. Real learning is an active question–answer process, and learning the process is as important as learning specific information.

2. Making students part of the feedback-evaluation system: The division of labor in the traditional feedback-evaluation system follows a standard pattern: students perform, teachers grade their performance. Three basic premises underlie the system:

1. That teachers somehow "own" what they teach and, to maintain its value, must guard and ration it
2. That an evaluation is tainted if those evaluated participate
3. That learning, like meat or eggs, requires impartial oversight and standardized grades

The system, of course, fosters anxiety. The greater the separation between judge and judged, the greater the potential for distress; and the longer the lapse between performance and evaluation, the longer tension builds and fear takes hold. Students may feel helpless. If they suspect negative results—a failing grade or punishment—they may also feel hopeless or apathetic—all reactions that interrupt and may even reverse active learning patterns.

Because they contribute to anxiety, which in turn impedes learning, I do not believe in D and F grades for elementary school students studying mathematics. Certainly, teachers must conform to the grading systems adopted by their schools. However, I have found a workable compromise for day-to-day activities is to grade passing work A, B, or C and not-passing work KW for keep working. Without the immediate threat of failure and its consequences, students develop a climb-the-mountain determination. Because they know the mountain will still be there tomorrow and the only way over is up, they tend to work harder and more confidently.

That confidence is a response in part at least to a message implicit in the A, B, C, KW system: it says clearly that the teacher not only believes that everyone can learn math but also expects everyone to learn and pass with an A, B, or C grade. To this confidence in students' abilities, we should add confidence in their integrity and make students part of the evaluation process.

Having students grade their own exercises and quizzes, assess their own progress, or set their own goals has two immediate consequences. First, it frees the teacher from the monotonous chore of marking hundreds of tests per term. Second, it reduces the time between performance and feedback, enabling students themselves to accelerate the learning cycle. Even more importantly, it puts students in the proprietary loop. Because they are in control of information sources, they in effect "own" the information and, oddly enough, will often be more stringent in applying standards to themselves than their teachers would be.

Will some students cheat? Perhaps. But cheating does not come naturally to children and, if it occurs, it is usually a sign of desperation. If there is no cause to be desperate—no failing grades, punishments, feelings of helplessness and hopelessness—students are more likely to be honest with themselves and their teachers.

Developing Learning-Friendly Classroom Relationships

Recently, a teacher who prides herself on motivating students to learn math described her favorite math game to me. She calls it the Math Bee. As in an old-fashioned spelling bee, student captains choose their teams based on math performance ("I want Suzanne because she always gets A's in math." "I'll take George if you'll take Sam." "I don't want Coleen—she gets D's.") Then the teacher "throws" problems out to be solved. Mental calculations result in double points. Students return to their seats when they make errors. The team with the last member standing wins.

This teacher was extremely proud of her Math Bee because, as she explained, "It lights a fire under the slower students and makes the good students fierce competitors." It also, from my own observations, creates adversarial relationships among classmates, places at-risk students in no-win situations, and makes the teacher a referee rather than a teacher.

Is there a place for competition in an anxiety-free math class? Yes. But the competition that promotes eustress rather than distress is self-directed; this means students compete against themselves instead of against each other. They try to improve their highest score, achieve mastery on the first try, complete more learning units in less time. Because no one loses in self-directed competition, there are fewer opportunities for distress and more opportunities for eustress. And because there is nothing to be gained by out-performing classmates, students are free to help each other, pool their knowledge, and collaborate on problem solving.

1. *Collaborative-learning:* The importance of students' working together to solve problems has become an axiom of modern math teaching. The basic principle is simple but sound: Two heads (or three or four or five) are generally better than one. The method also works to minimize anxiety because the responsibility as well as the task is shared.

To be truly collaborative, the learning process must involve everyone—both students in learning partnerships, all of the students in small groups or class activities. There is always the danger, of course, that the more aggressive students will do all of the work, carrying the other students rather than collaborating with them. For this reason, grouping students for collaboration may run contrary to the standard practice of selecting for complementary skills—aggressive with passive, strong with weak, math confident with math timid. In fact, pairing a passive student with another passive student or a math-timid student with another math-timid student increases the opportunity for both to contribute; and pairing strong, confident, or aggressive students ensures that no one student will dominate. In addition, assigning one concept to a group but different problems to individual members helps rotate the leadership in problem solving because students tend to take the initiative—presenting the problem, trying to understand it, seeking ways to solve it—on problems assigned directly to them.

2. *Self-actualizing goals:* While grading on a curve may have its uses, I prefer grading by standards in math courses. Once a general goal is set for the entire class to reach—often 80 percent or higher if you use a mastery system—then individual goals can be presented as a ladder or stepping stones, leading the students from wherever they are now to wherever they need to be in terms of the class standards. Again, the students compete only against themselves so that destructive rivalries and potentially demeaning class standings are avoided. Self-actualizing goals and set standards for achievement work well with collaborative learning. Students have no reason not to cooperate and every reason to help each other.

3. *The Pygmalion effect:* We have all heard of the hidden curriculum, the self-fulfilling prophecy, and the Pygmalion effect in the classroom. Usually studies emphasize negative effects, but the principles can work in the opposite direction as well. If the teacher believes all of the students can learn math, the students will believe that they, individually as well as collectively, can learn math. Setting high standards, presenting a challenging curriculum, avoiding the winner–loser system of curved grading, refusing to administer defeat by assigning D and F grades—all of these overt teaching behaviors carry a covert message to students: you are intelligent; you can learn math; you can excel in math; your teacher believes in you; you will succeed if you only keep trying; your teacher won't give up on you; you can't give up on yourself.

A good part of Jaime Escalante's success must be attributed to the Pygmalion effect. He believed in his students, and his belief convinced them to believe in themselves. Once that basic level of trust and acceptance was established, they could succeed at whatever task he set in front of them, including calculus.

I once assisted a school by developing instruments for assessing math performance at the various grade levels. The effect of different teaching philosophies on curriculum and achievement was almost immediately apparent. One group of teachers wanted simple pre- and posttests so that students would not be discouraged by poor performance. Teachers in that group taught the minimums because they did not believe the students were capable of learning more. The second group of teachers wanted difficult pre- and posttests to match their challenging curriculum.

Predictably, the students of the first group learned little math; the students of the second group, much more. Also predictably, developing assessment instruments that both groups could use proved impossible.

Debugging the Information-Processing System

What happens when a computer program develops a glitch? You debug it. To debug a program, you must look at its operation as a process. What happens first, second, and third; what leads to this response as opposed to that response and so forth. To find the glitches in a math class, we can begin by looking at the math learning process. Figure 5-4 on page 64 shows a traditional three-store model of information processing, whereas Figure 5-5 on page 65 applies the model to math learning. The model is not so much a scientific explanation of how information is processed as a visual representation. (Current research favors more complex models.)

Reading from left to right on Figure 5-4, information enters the system through stimuli that register in the first store, the Sensory Information Store. The learner selects which data to pay attention to, allowing the rest to decay. The second store, the Short-Term Memory Store, is the next stop, the learner's working memory or attention box. This is where the data are analyzed and interpreted and problems are solved. The third store, Long-Term Memory Store, provides information and skills needed to understand and process the material in working memory, as well as a storehouse for the results of learning. Moving up and left again, the Response Generator outputs results, such as a completed exercise or quiz paper or a spoken response to a question.

Figure 5-5 shows how the problem-solving process might look for a simple addition problem. If the teacher speaks the problem, writes it out, and poses it with manipulatives, the problem is introduced on three sensory registers—echoic (for auditory information), iconic (for visual information), and tactile (for touch/feel information). Paying attention to the problem puts it in working memory. Then the learner draws on previously learned information in long-term memory to identify the problem as one involving the operation of addition and application of this operation. Presenting the results of the process as a written sum, $3 + 2 = 5$, calls again on long-term memory for knowledge of numbers, knowledge of summation, and writing skills. At the same time the learner can file in long-term memory the equivalency of the problem's different forms.

Glitches can occur at any stage of processing. What if, for example, students are not paying attention? Often, when problems are presented in only one way, for example in written numbers, other stimuli interfere. The difficulty, then, is at the sensory register stage; debugging may consist of introducing information on several registers at once, as we did with the addition problem in Figure 5-5.

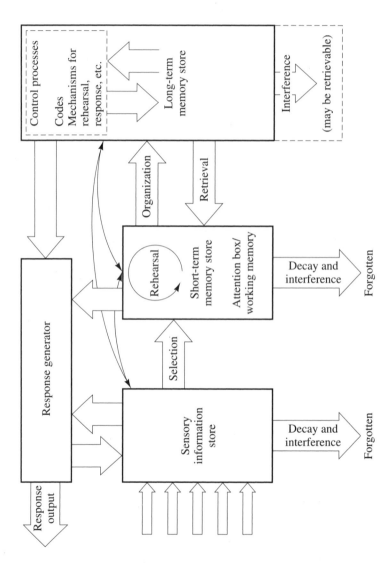

FIGURE 5-4 Multistore Model of Information Processing

Source: Adapted from A. Woolfolk, *Educational Psychology*, 6th ed., Figure 7-1, p. 244. Englewood Cliffs, NJ: Prentice-Hall, Inc., a Division of Simon and Schuster, 1995.

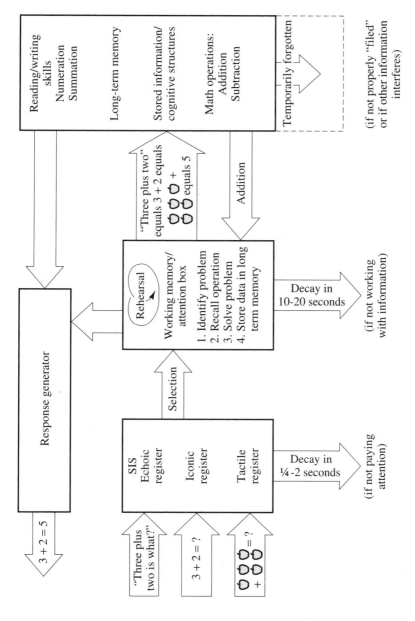

FIGURE 5-5   Processing Math Problems: Multistore Model of Information Processing

65

A common glitch at the working-memory stage happens when the process is interrupted. This is similar to turning off your computer without saving your work: the work is lost. Minimizing interruptions from announcements or distractions, pacing instruction with frequent backups of summary and integration, repeating and rephrasing information, and allowing sufficient time to complete work—all are effective countermeasures because they keep the process moving, and continuous action is necessary to keep information alive in the attention box.

Rote learning creates processing glitches associated specifically with long-term memory. Imagine a filing cabinet with hundreds of files but no filing system. The result is the same when information is learned by rote rather than with meaning; everything is there in long-term memory, but there is no meaningful system of organization that allows you to find and retrieve it. "Debugging" these glitches begins with the curriculum. Teaching concepts in a meaningful context, emphasizing idea patterns and relationships, connecting new information to old, and using mnemonic techniques provide structures for remembering and improving retrieval.

How about the student who works problems diligently and correctly during class but the next day has forgotten how to solve them? The difficulty probably lies with transferring information from short-term memory to long-term memory. Or the student who slowly reads and rereads a problem without starting to solve it? There may be interference on the sensory register, or the slowness of the reading could be allowing the student's mind to wander.

How well students process information determines to a great extent how well and how much they learn. When the processing flow is blocked at any point, the result will be errors, misunderstood and half-understood ideas, and ultimately frustration and anxiety.

Changing Distress to Eustress

Finally, to create an anxiety-free but productive math class, it is not enough simply to remove the sources of distress; we must replace them with sources of eustress. Several years ago I was teaching a remedial math class filled with math-anxious students. At the beginning of the class, my goal was tolerance. If I could teach some math and persuade the students to tolerate math, I would have been satisfied, but I did not get far with those modest objectives. It was not until I decided to teach a lot of math and persuade the students to love math that I saw incredible results: that is, I shifted from simply eliminating negative learning patterns and attitudes to replacing them with positive patterns and attitudes. Most of the students in that basic course eventually enrolled in my calculus course, and some even became math majors who completed one or more degrees in mathematics over the following years.

Use the following chart as a distress/eustress checklist. A distressful class will necessarily be a math-anxious class, whereas a eustressful class will be, potentially at least, a math confident and a math-competent class.

Classroom Stress

Distress	*Eustress*
No-win situations	Win–win challenges
Impossible challenges	Possible challenges
Threat of failure	Promise of success
I-can't attitude	I-can attitude
Helplessness, hopelessness	Helpfulness, hopefulness
Distrustful classroom relationships	Trustful classroom relationships
You're-on-your-own class structure	We're-in-it-together class structure
Negative motivators	Positive motivators
Not knowing	Knowing
Flawed information processing	Effective information processing
Limited access to knowledge	Unlimited access to knowledge
No control of learning	Control of learning
They-can't-do-it teaching	They-can-do-it teaching
Static learning dynamics	Active learning dynamics
Know-your-limits thinking	Know-no-limits thinking

Questions for Thought and Discussion

1. How important is the physical structure of the math class to learning? How might physical structure and learning structure differ?

2. How valid is this statement: Math learning increases with determination, but decreases with desperation?

3. What is the dividing line between productive and nonproductive chaos in the math classroom?

4. Recall math classes you have observed or been enrolled in. Which ones were most enjoyable? Most productive? Were the most enjoyable ones also the most productive?

Activities

1. Observe several math class sessions and chart the dynamics. If possible, observe different types of math classes, including at least one traditonal and one nontraditional classroom.

2. Use the model in Figure 5-5 to diagram the processing of some specific information you are learning. At what stages are you processing the information effectively? Where and how might you improve?

3. Develop a series of lesson plans to replace specific, distressful influences in a math class with eustressful influences.

Annotated List of Readings

Selye, Hans. *The Stress of Life*. New York: McGraw-Hill, 1956, 1975. *Classic work on stress psychology. Covers personal research leading to the discovery of the general adaptation syndrome.*

Selye, Hans. *Stress without Distress*. New York: J. B. Lippincott, 1974. *Popularized treatment of Selye's stress research. Makes important distinctions between distress and eustress.*

Biehler, Robert E., and Jack Snowman. *Psychology Applied to Teaching,* 7th ed. Boston: Houghton Mifflin, 1993. *Readable chapter on information-processing theory. Focuses on applications to classroom situations and pays special attention to the cognitive and affective domains.*

6

Matching Instruction to Cognitive Levels

"What's your favorite subject?" I asked a group of fifth-graders recently.

"I like math, but I hate fractions," one youngster told me.

"And long division," added another.

"And percents," said a third, "and multiplying with two numbers."

Why should youngsters who have mastered addition and subtraction dislike multiplication and division? Why should youngsters who are comfortable with whole numbers be uncomfortable with fractions or decimals or percentages? In fact, why should youngsters who enjoy working with numbers have trouble with any arithmetical operations?

The questions are simpler than the answers. Fifth-graders are for the most part functioning at the cognitive level Piaget calls *concrete operational.* They are young scientists. They like to work with the tangible before they come to conclusions, and they ask for concrete referents in answer to their questions. Although all arithmetical operations are well within the scope of these youngsters' cognitive level, traditional pedagogy is better suited to the next stage in cognitive development, the level of formal operations or abstract thinking.

Take, for example, the problem $1/2 + 1/4 + 1/4 = 1$. We can give the problem concrete referents if we start with a broken pie and add pieces to the pie one at a time.

| 1/2 | + | 1/4 | + | 1/4 | = | 1 |

But most teachers will not approach the problem in that way; some might even say that this makes the problem too easy (in the same way that using the fingers and toes makes counting too easy). Instead, they will tell students first to find a common denominator for 1/2 and 1/4, then to change all fractions so that they have the same denominator, next to add numerators while keeping denominators the same, and finally to reduce the sum to a whole number. In other words, teachers will take a simple problem with easily imagined concrete referents and make it into a complex problem with many levels of abstraction. The problem itself is well within the range of concrete-operational thinking, but the pedagogy is more appropriate for formal-operational thinking—a cognitive level that some may not reach for another five to ten years.

The immediate result is frustration. Students may imitate the process with some success, even working problems and getting correct answers at least part of the time. But they do not really understand what they are doing, and this lack of understanding leaves gaps in basic knowledge and undermines self-confidence—both of which are contributing factors in math anxiety.

To avoid frustration and its effects, teachers must match pedagogy and curriculum to their students' readiness to learn. To do that, we need a clear understanding of not only how children learn but also what they can learn and when they can learn it.

Piaget's Stage Theory of Development

Several theories of intellectual development have merit, but Jean Piaget's stage theory continues to be the most useful for teachers. During more than forty years of research, Piaget's ideas have been not only supported but also applied directly to education in literally hundreds of studies in dozens of countries. Both the stages themselves and progression through the stages have been found to be universal and cross-cultural; therefore, they can be used to interpret and to predict learning behaviors of youngsters from a variety of ethnic and racial backgrounds. Moreover, because Piaget's theory is specifically a theory of the development of mathematical logic, applications to teaching math are direct and clear.

Piaget describes four different stages in a child's intellectual development: sensory-motor, preoperational, concrete operational, and formal operational. At each stage, children select information and interact with their environments in different ways. Figure 6-1 on pages 72–73 shows some of the characteristics of learning at each stage as well as some approximate ages for the stages. Although the ages may vary from group to group and even from individual to individual, progression from stage to stage does not. That is, a child interacting with the environment on the sensory-motor level will not suddenly leap to concrete operations or a child in the preoperational stage to formal operations. Development occurs from sensory-motor to preoperational to concrete operational to formal operational.

What does this mean for the teacher? Are we faced with teaching every concept in four different ways? Not really. Because children may progress through the stages at different rates but not in different orders, chances are that the range of development in any one class will be narrow enough that targeting the middle of the range will keep instruction within reach of the whole class. As we will discuss later, the distance from the bottom to the top of the range can be bridged effectively by using those at the top as peer tutors for those at the bottom.

The best way to think of the stages is not as benchmarks or milestones but as potentials. When a child's development enters the concrete-operational stage, that means the potential exists for that child to learn about geometric shapes and to think empirically, using concrete applications to test hypotheses. This does not mean that the child automatically knows these things or has automatically mastered these thinking skills. The potential exists, but whether and to what extent that potential develops depends on several things, including the availability of appropriate learning materials, the use of teaching methods that match the stage, and the amount of time devoted to the systematic and thorough investigations essential for concrete-operational learning.

In other words, a child's intellectual development is the result of an interaction between what the child brings to learning and what the learning environment provides. For the child's intellectual potential to be reached, the environment must match the child's readiness to learn. For the child to learn math initially, we may need to throw away our chalkboards, forget about pencil-and-paper exercises, and make numbers real. When they see numbers as real, concrete-operational thinkers will be better prepared to learn from the more abstract presentations provided by chalkboards and paper-and-pencil work.

Although the predominant stages for kindergarten through elementary school are preoperational and concrete operational, surveying all four stages will help us see development as a coherent process that in a sense organizes and even regulates math learning.

Math and the Sensory-Motor Stage

Piaget estimated that the sensory-motor stage would last from birth to around age two. Babies learn by using their senses and muscles. They look; they touch; they taste; they listen; they smell. Although they might not be ready for learning math directly, they are beginning to develop skills that will be important later on when they are introduced to numbers.

Two important skills developed in this stage involve distinguishing between objects and gaining a sense of object permanence. Babies, as every parent knows (and deplores), often "think" with their mouths: everything goes in. Good taste and bad taste help the baby experience directly what belongs and what does not belong there while parents reinforce or supplement these discoveries with "No-no," "Yes,"

FIGURE 6-1   Piaget's Stages of Development Applied to Math Instruction

	Sensory-Motor	*Preoperational*
Definition	Stage of learning related to muscle movements and sensory inputs	Thinking by infralogical or prelogical operations
Key Characteristics	—Information collected through senses —Direct physical action used to explore environment —Rudiments of language development —Egocentricity	—Imitative behavior —Continued "I"-centered thinking —Enhanced language development paired with increase in use of symbols —Heightened creativity
What to Learn	—Object discrimination —Object permanence —Sense of time and space	—Measurement —Seriation —Counting —Classification —Combining
How to Learn	—Play activities with blocks to develop hand-and-eye coordination and to learn to discriminate among different shapes, colors, and sizes Peek-a-boo/now-you see-it-now-you-don't games to develop sense of object permanence —Sensory experiences—mobiles, listening activities, tasting activities to aid discrimination	—See-do-and-tell activities —Building projects —Life-skill projects such as cooking, shopping, sewing —Games that call for counting, classifying, etc.
Age Range	Birth–2 years	2–7 years

or "Good, baby." Babies and toddlers also go through several stages in learning that a person or object can exist without being physically present. All parents will recognize the familiar sequence: baby is quiet; parent leaves the room; baby cries; parent comes back; baby is quiet again. According to one brand of nursing wisdom, the baby is spoiled and should be ignored; what is happening, however, is neither capricious nor meaningless. At an unconscious level, the baby is experimenting

Concrete-Operational	*Formal-Operational*
Thought patterns rooted in tangible objects but becoming orderly and internal via logical operations	Thought liberated from tangible; potential for development of complex, logical mental systems
—Empirical learning —Step-by-step reasoning —Dualistic (either/or) thinking —Development of internal but weak thought structures —Realism	—Reasoning from hypotheses —Development of value systems —Idealism —Decentralized thinking —Ability to synthesize —Deductive logic —Reflective thinking —Complex abstract thought
—Addition/subtraction —Multiplication/Division —Fractions —Decimals —Percentages	—Geometry —Algebra —Trigonometry —Calculus —Postcalculus content areas
—Laboratory-field experience activities —Explore-invent-discover learning sets —Repetition and verbalization to reinforce weak thought patterns —Computer activities that include strong visuals	—Bridge activities in early stages which move from the concrete to the abstract —Explore-invent-discover learning sets —Combination of paper-and-pencil work with computer applications that provide immediate and detailed feedback
7–12 years	12+ years

with object permanence. When the sequence has been repeated many times with the same result, the parent's return, the baby will have learned that the parent still exists even when out of sight.

Both of these skills—distinguishing between objects and exploring object permanence—are critical for future math learning because they are fundamental to the processes that will allow the child to understand the concepts of number and arithmetic operations. Encouraging their development through methods like those listed in Figure 6-1 will prepare the child for the true beginning of math learning in the preoperational stage.

Math and the Preoperational Stage

The preoperational stage extends from approximately age two to age seven, with some overlap with the sensory-motor and concrete-operational stages at the extremes of the range. This is the intuitive stage. Logical processes, such as the arithmetic operations, are still out of reach, but critical thinking is beginning. Language development during this stage accelerates, and creativity appears, often in the form of fantasies as in the creation of an invisible friend.

Because preoperational children are beginning to develop attitudes and values, the stage is crucial to the affective dimension of math learning. If early preoperational children are pressured to do chalkboard arithmetic, they may use imitative rather than logical skills to achieve an appearance of success while at the same time they begin to erect the complex structure of negative feelings, experiences, and expectations that constitute math anxiety. On the other hand, when preoperational children are introduced to math concepts appropriate to their level of development, they begin to develop math courage—confidence in what they already know and willingness to face the challenge of more difficult concepts.

Specifically, this is the stage for learning to count and measure, to tell time, to work with series and hierarchies, and to begin combining activities essential to addition. Throughout the stage children are using spoken language as a primary vehicle for learning; therefore, it is important to verbalize extensively. Not only should the teacher explain and explain again, but also the children should explain what they are doing, what they think the teacher is doing, why they are doing it, how they are doing it, and so forth. The following learning scenarios illustrate the progression in complexity as children move through the preoperational stage, as well as the way learning of new ideas builds on previous understanding.

Scenario #1: Ages 2–3

Lesson: Quantity, How much?

Setting: Preschool playroom. Children sit on floor in circle around teacher.

Materials: Bags of multicolored marbles

Dialogue:

Teacher *(spilling a bag of marbles on the floor):* What do I have here?
Children *(catching marbles as they roll around the floor):* Marbles!
Teacher: What kind of marbles?

Children: Blue marbles!
        Green marbles!
        Red!
        Yellow!
Teacher: Do I have a lot of marbles?
Children: Yes.
        No.
        Yes.
Teacher *(spilling more marbles on the floor):* Do I have more marbles now?
Children: Yes!
Teacher *(putting some marbles back in bag):* How about now?
Children: Yes!
        No!
Teacher *(spilling all the marbles on the floor):* Now?
Children: More!
Teacher *(bagging all but a few marbles):* Now? Do I still have a lot of marbles?
Children: No!
Teacher: What happens if I pour all the marbles into two piles, one pile in front of Kim and one pile in front of José? Who has the most marbles?
Children: Kim has most!
Teacher: Why?
Children: Kim's pile is bigger!
Teacher: What if I take some marbles from Kim's pile and put them into José's pile? Now who has the bigger pile?
Children: José!
Teacher: Are you sure? They look about the same to me.

Scenario #2: Age 4

Lesson: Counting, How many?

Setting: Preschool playroom. Children sit around the worktable.

Materials: Large box of marbles. Teacher puts two marbles in front of each child, then holds up a marble in each hand.

Dialogue:

Teacher: This marble is number one. This marble is number two. Now count your marbles in the same way.
Children: Marble one, marble two.
Teacher: Now I am taking another marble from the box. This marble is number three. *(Teacher continues, increasing the number of marbles to ten, then works backward.)*

Scenario #3: Age 5-6

Lesson: Combining, How many?

Setting: Kindergarten classroom. Children sit around worktable.

Materials: Large box of marbles. Teacher puts several marbles in front of each child, taking care not to give all the same number of marbles.

Dialogue:

Teacher: Count the marbles in front of you. How many do you have?
Children: One-two-three-four marbles.
          One-two marbles.
          One-two-three marbles.
Teacher *(giving each child another marble):* Now how many do you have? *(Teacher continues adding marbles, telling the children to stop when each has ten.)* Now count out two marbles from your ten and put them on your left. Now count out three marbles from the ones left and put them on your right. Now put the two marbles and the three marbles together. How many do you have?

Although it is important at this stage and the next to emphasize hands-on learning, children may benefit most from verbalizing what they are doing. Dialogues like those in the lesson scenarios are, of course, only one method of verbalizing. Another is to write out the operations in words and numbers. Counting skills, introduced at the beginning of the stage, can be reinforced and strengthened throughout the stage by periodically extending the number range, by adding (when the child is learning to write) the written to the spoken word, and by introducing Arabic numerals as another type of number symbol. Similarly, combining skills can be supported by written work with both words and numerals. However, care must be taken not to let pencil-and-paper or even computerized lessons and exercises supplant object-based activities.

Looking back at the preceding scenarios, can we say that after the series of counting and combining lessons, the children understand the fundamentals of number and addition? Probably not. But they have begun to organize their experiences with objects in a way that will prepare them to understand.

Math and the Concrete-Operational Stage

Operations, as Piaget defines them, "concern transformations of reality by means of internalized actions that are grouped into coherent, reversible systems (joining and separating, etc.)" (Piaget and Inhelder 1969, p. 93). Concrete operations start with concrete objects rather than abstract ideas. They provide what Piaget calls a "transition between schemes of action and the general logical structures . . ." that characterize thinking during the formal-operational stage (Piaget and Inhelder 1969, p. 100).

Generally, the potentials and parameters of learning at this stage begin to develop around age seven or eight and continue into early adolescence. (However, some research suggests that the learning and thinking patterns typical of the stage may continue into adulthood.) Asked about their favorite school subject, many concrete-operational children will reply, "Math." Mathematics calls for the step-by-step reasoning characteristic of thinking during this stage, and basic concepts and operations match the stage's thought structures closely. For example, addition, subtraction, multiplication, and division rely on internalizing experiences with combining and separating objects. Moreover, throughout the stage the child progresses rapidly in understanding the concept of number; that is, we see a progressive synthesis of the mental constructs called *inclusion* and *seriation*. On the other hand, the child is learning that *one* may refer to one tree, one horse, or one hand, while at the same time understanding that we can order a group of ten trees by numbering them in a series: one, two, three, and so forth. Because mathematical concepts match the readiness of children at this stage to learn them, learning math may be as satisfying to concrete-operational children as learning language was during the highly verbal preoperational stage—hence the tendency to cite math as a favorite subject.

Potentially, then, the concrete-operational stage should be a time for accelerated learning of both math and science. At the same time, however, a mismatching at this stage of concepts and pedagogy can lead to the kind of learning short-circuits typified by the fifth-graders mentioned at the beginning of this chapter. Although fractions, decimals, and long division are well within these children's developmental abilities, teaching them abstractly rather than concretely leaves gaps in the step-by-step construction of a coherent mental system.

To avoid the short circuits and to take advantage of concrete-operational children's propensity for learning math, pedagogy must meet three key tests: (1) Does it fill in the gaps? (2) Does it make numbers real (that is, does it show rather than tell)? (3) Does it foster problem-solving behaviors rather than repetitive, imitative actions?

1. *Filling in the gaps:* Although the connections between concepts may seem obvious to an adult, children at this stage require a greater degree of explicitness. For example, it is not enough simply to say that multiplication extends the concept of addition, and then to teach multiplication as a separate operation with a distinct set of rules. Ideally, children should be led through the extension themselves as in the following learning scenario.

Scenario #4: Age 8–9

Lesson: Multiplying to Add/Adding to Multiply

Materials: Bags of pinto beans. Teacher gives each child a small bag of beans.

Activities:

   a. Teacher asks the children to count out three stacks of beans with five beans in each stack, then five stacks of beans with three beans in each stack. After the children have counted the total number of beans in each set, the teacher has them represent the activity as an addition problem: $5 + 5 + 5 = 15$ and $3 + 3 + 3 + 3 + 3 = 15$.

   b. After activity "a" has been repeated several times with different numbers of beans, the teacher asks the children to explain what they are doing, first leading them step by step to discover the similarity between the problem of adding five threes and adding three fives, and then introducing 5×3 and 3×5 as another way to write the problem.

   c. To explore the relationship between addition and multiplication further, children return to the piles of pinto beans. Asked to solve the problem 4×2 and 2×4, they first prepare four piles of two beans each and two piles of four beans each, then check their answers by rewriting the problem as addition: $2 + 2 + 2 + 2 = 8$ or $4 + 4 = 8$.

   2. Making numbers real: How to make numbers real is explored at length in another chapter, but the rationale for anchoring math learning in activities with tangible objects depends on the nature of concrete-operational thinking. Although logical structures are developing during this stage, they are relatively weak. They need the reinforcement of sense data. If the children can see and do as well as think—that is, if they can add direct physical action to mental action—the effect will be a coherent, cohesive mental system. In the multiplication lesson described here, the beans allow students to feel and see the problem; moreover, by beginning their study of multiplication empirically, many of the children will discover the basic principles of the operation for themselves and consequently will feel greater confidence in their knowledge. Scenario #5 illustrates a similar approach to fractions—beginning with activities that show the relationship of fractions to division.

Scenario #5: Age 10–11

Lesson: Working with Fractions

Materials: Colored paper wheels. Teacher gives each child a stack of wheels and scissors.

Activities:

   a. Teacher has students fold a wheel twice and cut along the folds, then asks: "How many parts have you divided the wheel into? Can you write that as a division problem?"

b. After activity "a" has been repeated several times with different numbers, the teacher introduces the fraction as another way to represent division, explaining that "1/2 says that you divide one by two and 2/3 says that you divide two by three." Students then explore the meaning of a variety of fractions, first by cutting paper wheels and then by writing them out in both numbers and words.

c. The cut-up parts of the paper wheels also provide a starting point to study adding fractions. The teacher asks students to find four halves or eight fourths and fit them together. After students have assembled two whole wheels, they can experiment with representing their actions with fractions: 1/2 + 1/2 + 1/2 + 1/2 = 4/2 = 2; 1/4 + 1/4 + 1/4 + 1/4 + 1/4 + 1/4 + 1/4 + 1/4 = 8/4 = 2.

Of course, making numbers real becomes more difficult as the numbers become larger and the problems more complex. Fortunately, computer programs have been developed to provide visuals for arithmetic procedures, and these can be integrated effectively into a curriculum that emphasizes hands-on activities so that students can continue to "see" tangible referents for numbers and procedures.

3. *Problem-solving behaviors:* Ensuring a problem-solving rather than an imitative approach in math learning depends heavily on both the step-by-step approach that systematically builds conceptual structures and the hands-on activities that make numbers real. Some obvious clues to imitative learning include errors when problems are taken out of sequence or when there is a variation in the way a problem is presented or in some of the operations required. For example, if students get one answer for $4\overline{)124}$ and another for 124/4, they are imitating procedures rather than solving problems. Problem-solving strategies for concrete-operational children should begin with making a problem that is presented in numbers or words tangible. That means allowing children to manipulate Cuisenaire rods, marbles, beans, or fingers and toes—whatever it takes for them to grasp and grapple with the problem.

Scenario #6: Age 11–12

Lesson: Word Problems (students work in groups)

Materials: Tape measure, home furnishings catalog

Activities:

a. You have $1,000 to spend on a carpet and pad for your classroom. Measure the classroom floor to find out how many square yards of carpeting and padding will be needed. Then use the catalogs to find which carpet you can afford. Be careful to include any installation costs in your calculations.

b. There are three windows in this classroom. Use the tape measure to determine their size. Then use the catalogs to determine the cost of installing new blinds at one, two, and three windows.

c. Find the cost of wallpapering one of the walls of this classroom. Measure the area of the wall overall; then subtract the area of any obstructions such as chalkboards or doors.

Notice that each word problem requires some physical action and then several mathematical operations. Moreover, each problem may have several solutions since groups may choose different products in the catalogs. This provides an effective safeguard against rote responses as well as an opportunity to reinforce effective problem solving in class discussions of results.

Math and the Formal Operational Stage

If concrete-operational thinkers with their predilection for experimentation are called "young empiricists" or "young scientists," then we might call formal operations the stage of "young philosophers." When youngsters will begin to show potential for the kinds of logical processes that constitute abstract thinking depends to some extent on how well they have realized the potentials of the concrete-operational stage. We might say that when youngsters no longer need to rely on the tangible to keep their thinking on track, they are entering the stage of formal operations. Usually this begins to happen during preadolescence and continues throughout the adolescent years.

In terms of the math curriculum, geometry rather than algebra may be the ideal transitional subject. Referents are concrete. Youngsters will already have been introduced to many concepts and procedures, such as calculating area or working with spatial relationships, and computer programs that use graphic illustrations provide an effective bridge from hands-on activities. In addition, work with derivations and axioms takes the step-by-step reasoning students favored during the concrete-operational stage to a new level of complexity and prepares the way for the more abstract reasoning involved in algebra.

Unfortunately, many math programs introduce algebra before geometry. Instead of making a smooth transition, object-centered thinking is exchanged abruptly for idea-centered thinking. The more advanced student may make the leap successfully, but the less advanced will flounder. "But what do x and y mean?" students complain, or "Why do we have to learn algebra? We'll never use it in real life." Because their thought mechanisms are not ready for the kind of thinking required, the subject is incomprehensible at a conceptual level; they may achieve some appearance of success by imitating procedures, but they do not really understand what they are doing. Moreover, the students know they do not understand. The result, of course, is math anxiety.

During early adolescence, the math curriculum should lead students in a steady progression from object-centered to object-free thinking. However, teachers still must be sensitive to clues that newly forming mental structures are weakening. Comments that appear to be peripheral or illogical—for example, questions about concrete referents for variables—could indicate a break in the conceptual chain and the need to retrace some ground.

The Lawson and Renner Method

As I mentioned earlier, the stages in thought development described in this chapter are not discrete units of information and skills that may be mastered out of order or in smorgasbord style—a little of this, a little of that, and so forth. Development is a progression. It moves by increments, with successive mental structures building on those developed previously and forming a foundation for those to be developed in the future.

To help rather than hinder development, teaching must be systematic and thorough. Concepts should never be taught in isolation but presented as extensions of previously mastered information. A strategy developed by Lawson and Renner (1975) provides an effective pedagogical match. Their three-phase procedure guides students in (1) exploring the concepts, (2) inventing mental structures to deal with the concepts, and (3) discovering applications of the concepts in a variety of contexts.

Teachers can apply this procedure by organizing lessons in learning sets. Each set demonstrates a specific idea or relationship for students to explore. The order of the activities or exercises in each set leads students to "invent," or formulate for themselves, the concept implicit in the set—a process that teachers can reinforce with explanations and additional examples. Each succeeding set should reinforce concepts learned in the preceding set and broaden the students' understanding as they discover new applications.

Instruction should begin with what the students already know, the familiar, then gradually build to new concepts and applications. For example, Figure 6-2 on page 82 illustrates sets of activities designed to teach preoperational children the Commutative Law of Addition. The children move from the activity of combining physical objects in the first set, to combining visual objects in the second set, to working with words and numbers in the final set. Throughout the activities, children should verbalize both physical and mental actions—explaining to the teacher, to each other, or even to themselves what they are doing and why they are doing it.

Figure 6-3 on page 83 illustrates other sets of activities for teaching the Commutative Law of Addition—this time designed for the concrete-operational level and the study of fractions. The initial activity roots learning firmly in the concrete; then successive learning sets lead students toward more complex manipulations, including reversing addition in subtraction.

Actual physical objects	To be verbalized by teacher and students	
	Visual representations	Symbolic Equivalents
These can be any familiar objects, such as coins, chips, apples, oranges, marbles, popsicle sticks, etc.	$O + O = OO$	$1 + 1 = 2$
	$O + OO = OOO$	$1 + 2 = 3$
Design problems corresponding to the ones in the set under visual representations.	$OO + O = OOO$	$2 + 1 = 3$
	$OO + OO = OOOO$	$2 + 2 = 4$
	$OO + OOO = OOOOO$	$2 + 3 = 5$
	$OOO + OO = OOOOO$	$3 + 2 = 5$

FIGURE 6-2   Preoperational Application: Commutative Law of Addition

The explore-invent-discover strategy works well at all levels of math instruction (I have used it successfully in courses from arithmetic to calculus). In terms of the Piagetian model, the Lawson-Renner method promotes mental development by responding directly to natural processes. It starts by matching tasks and present knowledge, then guides students through a series of disequilibrium experiences that require accommodations and the gradual building of more complex mental systems to deal with the more complex applications. Some guidelines for creating similar learning sets follow:

1. Work from the familiar to the unfamiliar and from the simple to the complex.
2. Focus on one idea at a time, using that idea as a constant throughout the set or series of sets.
3. Use repetition to emphasize relationships and to highlight differences.
4. Increase complexity incrementally by sequencing steps that provide for a pattern of thinking, thereby strengthening the gradual climb toward understanding.
5. Write several sets of activities or exercises for key concepts to demonstrate different applications and perspectives.

Should be verbalized by teacher and students

Actual physical objects	Visual representations	Symbolic Equivalents
Any familiar object that can be divided into identifiable parts, such as apples, grapefruit, a pie, a cake, Cuisenaire rods, etc.		

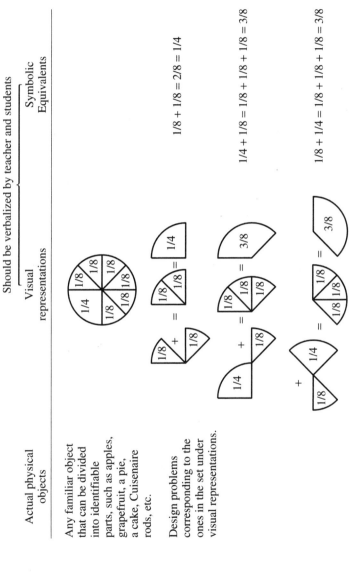

1/8 + 1/8 = 2/8 = 1/4

1/4 + 1/8 = 1/8 + 1/8 + 1/8 = 3/8

1/8 + 1/4 = 1/8 + 1/8 + 1/8 = 3/8

Design problems corresponding to the ones in the set under visual representations.

FIGURE 6-3 Concrete-Operational Application: Commutative Law of Addition with Fractions

83

6. Ask students to verbalize their mental processes, either aloud or on paper, to ensure understanding.

7. Troubleshoot for false learning. This includes instances of exclusively imitative responding or responses generated by rote learning.

Questions for Thought and Discussion

1. In what ways does the current math curriculum in your school match students' readiness to learn? In what ways do the curriculum and students' readiness to learn not match?

2. What types of hands-on math activities are best suited for preoperational and for concrete-operational children?

3. What problems might you anticipate in making numbers real for fifth- or sixth-graders? How might you solve those problems?

4. Some educators insist that making learning easy sabotages a desirable outcome of education: the building of character as children struggle with difficult subjects. Do you agree or disagree? Why?

Activities

1. Develop a learning set of activities to teach concrete-operational children, who already understand decimals, about percentages.

2. Develop a learning set of activities to teach second-graders (late preoperational or early concrete-operational) to subtract.

Annotated List of Readings

Copeland, Richard W. *Learning Mathematics: Teaching Implications of Piaget's Research,* 4th ed. New York: Macmillan, 1984. *Focuses on how children learn from a Piagetian theoretical perspective. Emphasizes diagnostics to determine what type of mathematics the child is ready to learn rather than how to teach specific concepts.*

Gorman, Richard M. *Discovering Piaget: A Guide for Teachers.* Columbus, OH: Charles E. Merrill, 1972. *An introduction to Piagetian thought minus the usual jargon. Emphasis on applications rather than theory or research.*

Lawson, Anton E., and John W. Renner. "Piagetian Theory and Biology Teaching." *American Biology Teacher* 37 (September, 1975): 336–343. *Application of Piagetian theory in a three-phase, integrated teaching strategy.*

Piaget, Jean, and Barbel Inhelder. *The Psychology of the Child,* trans. Helen Weaver. New York: Basic Books, 1969. *Summary of Piaget's work and guide to the various stages of mental growth—basic characteristics and implications for learning as well as social interaction.*

7

Making Numbers Real— or Discovering Reality in Numbers

We live numbered lives. We are born on numbered dates; live in numbered houses in number-coded areas; talk to each other on numbered phones; and conduct the business of our lives with account numbers, policy numbers, social security numbers, PIN numbers, ID numbers, serial numbers, production numbers, sales numbers, and credit and debit numbers in an endless stream of transactions numbered by quantity, type, and time.

We measure our lives with numbers. Birth weight, birth height, the number of years we have lived, the number of children we were raised with, the number of children we have raised, the amount of time we devote to various activities in the course of a day, a week, a month, a year, a decade, a lifetime—all of these are numbered units. All impact our perceptions of our quality of life. Some people rate their self-worth by the number of cars they own or the number of dollars they earn per annum; others, by the number of pounds they have lost; still others, by their numbered ranking in a class or society or competition.

Numbers define our position—whether we are first in line or second in command; our portion—whether we share 50/50 or 60/40; and our commitment—whether we give 100 percent or 50 percent or only 10 percent. Numbers rule our actions—up at 6:00 A.M. and off to work by 8:00 A.M.; regulate out diet—1700 calories, 1300 milligrams of sodium, 500 milligrams of Vitamin C; and price-tag our pleasures—$26.95 for a steak and crab dinner, $118 for a room at the Sheraton, $26,793 for a Jeep Grand Cherokee.

Little wonder people are intimidated by numbers! And little wonder that number anxieties—including math anxiety—plague a majority of adults.

Preventing these anxieties in children is predicated on making our numbered world a comfortable, nonthreatening environment. This means, first, demystifying and demythologizing numbers. An educator who claimed to "hate" numbers once told me, "Numbers are the Frankensteins of knowledge—created from our nightmares to threaten our sanity." Numbers, of course, are monstrous only to those who do not understand them, and making numbers real begins with making them understandable.

How do children understand numbers? There are two parts to this question:

1. What are the ways in which they can deal intellectually with numbers?
2. What do numbers actually mean to them?

The answer to the first question emerges directly from our discussion in the preceding chapter. Children deal with numbers, not as adults, but as children. Their cognitive development affects not only the way they process information but also how they select information to process. Moreover, past learning experiences help shape current learning experiences. Pose the same problem to students of different ages: How many apples are growing on our backyard tree? A five- or six-year-old, who has learned about seriation, might try to count the apples on the tree. A nine- or ten-year-old, who has learned about weights and measures, might pick the apples first, then box and weigh them. A teenager, who has studied geometry and trigonometry, might measure an accessible part of the tree, count the number of apples, then estimate the total volume and the total number of apples. The problem is constant, but the problem solvers' cognitive and educational development shapes their approaches to the problem and even the form of their solutions.

Similarly, the meaning of numbers—including their "realness"—varies with age and experience. To adults, the number of dollars they earn affects survival—whether they have enough money to pay bills, buy food, and so forth. To children, the number of dollars earned or given as allowances and gifts affects the margins rather than the center of their lives—how many collector cards, marbles, comic books, and treats they can buy rather than whether they will eat or have a home to live in. The difference is one of kind rather than degree, and the difference extends throughout the world of numbers. An adult, socially schooled to crave "the ecstasy of victory" and fear "the agony of defeat," values being number one; a child, who has not yet learned to compete, may value being first only as a means of gaining adult approval. Adults fear many numbers—age 40, high prices, high cholesterol, increasing weight, decreasing income. Children are born with none of these fears and acquire them only gradually as they learn to measure themselves against society's norms and life's timetables.

Making numbers real, then, means making them real to children. To do this calls for a shift in perspective and may require reassessing some popular tools, such as manufactured manipulatives, and some popular goals, such as teaching four- or five-year-olds to "make change."

Scenario #1

A group of pre-schoolers are sitting at a small table with their teacher. In front of each child is a pile of small change—pennies, nickels, and dimes.

The teacher begins the lesson with counting. First they count five pennies; then she introduces the nickel. Next they count ten pennies, and she introduces the dime.

Teacher: How many pennies in a nickel?
Students: Five!
Teacher: How many pennies in a dime?
Students: Five!
Teacher: Count again. How many pennies in a nickel?
Students: Five!
Teacher: How many pennies in a dime?
Students: Five!
Nine!
Eleventy-nine.

Scenario #2

Sixth-graders work at a table littered with multicolored manipulatives. A worksheet filled with word problems sits beside each student.

Teacher: Work out the problems by hand first, then on paper.
Students: What are these colored things for?
Teacher: They'll help you get a 'feel' for the problem.
Student: Can we do the problems on paper first?
Student: Yes, then we'll know what to do with the colored things.

In both cases, the teacher is attempting to give students a hands-on learning experience. Both attempts fail because the teachers misinterpret their students' point of view. The preschoolers are more interested in money words than in money numbers. The sixth-graders see the manipulatives not as a way to make word problems concrete, but as another type and level of abstraction.

Does this mean that using objects to teach math is a waste of time? No, it means we must match hands-on experiences to children's readiness to learn and to their perceptions of reality. The preschoolers are ready to learn vocabulary; they like the sound of *penny, nickel,* and *dime,* and enjoy experimenting with made-up words (like *eleventy-nine*). They are less ready to do addition and subtraction—both basic to "making change." The sixth-graders may still be young scientists, learning best by doing, but the manipulatives are not real to them. The rods are just "colored things." They are less real, as the sixth-graders understand reality, than the words on the worksheets. To the teacher, the lesson plan moves from the concrete, working with manipulatives, to the abstract, working with numbers; to the students, it moves from abstractions they can touch to abstractions they can read, and because of past learning experiences, the students are more comfortable with the latter.

Teachers who want to tie math lessons to the real world need first to answer some basic questions:

1. What is the range of cognitive development among your students?
2. Have past experiences shaped your students' math-learning styles?
3. Have past experiences affected your students' math-learning attitudes?
4. What current factors—including values, technology, game fads, and so forth—make up the context for their math learning?
5. What possibilities do the above pose for math-learning activities and materials? What limitations?

Recently, several books have been published advocating early business-math learning. The thesis of these books is essentially the same: Teaching children to handle money promotes financial responsibility and at the same time makes math real. Unfortunately, the books generally make no distinction between adults' and children's cognitive development, learning background, or values. Moreover, they define simple and complex survival skills and responsible behavior in terms of adults' rather than children's cognitive realities. Because "making change" is a simple money-use skill for adults, they recommend teaching four-year-olds, who are not ready cognitively for addition or subtraction, to make change. Because balancing the budget is a basic survival skill for adults, they recommend teaching elementary school children to manage the household expenses or do the grocery shopping. And because responsible money management for adults involves investing money wisely, they recommend teaching children to manage a portfolio of stocks and bonds.

Money is real to children, but household budgets and stocks and bonds are not the terms of most children's reality. Preschoolers may learn to count money; children in the early grades, to buy things with it; and children in the later grades, to earn money and budget it. But by and large, to children money is something they can feel in their pockets—not an abstract commodity credited and debited in financial accounts. For most children money is less real than the tangible things it represents—hours spent raking leaves or selling magazine subscriptions; dollars needed to buy computer or video games, signature athletic shoes, or rollerblades.

Teachers can begin their assessment of students' number worlds with cognitive development scales like Piaget's stages described in Chapter 6, math curricula, and academic records. However, understanding the way specific classes or specific students interpret their worlds in numbers calls for student-generated rather than system-generated data.

Discovering Numbers in the Real World

Ask preschoolers what numbers are important, and they might give you their ages, the number they can count to, or the time they eat lunch. Ask children in the early grades the same question, and they might reply again with their ages but also with street addresses, telephone numbers, or "911." Children in the later grades might respond with batting averages, dollar amounts needed for some coveted toy, win–loss records for their favorite sports teams, or their top scores for a popular video game. Numbers trivia collected in concept maps, logs, and art help define children's numbers realities and can suggest hands-on math activities that work.

Numbers and Math Maps

Concept mapping in some ways is the antithesis of standard evaluation systems. Traditional testing measures children's grasp of concepts from the teacher's and the curriculum's viewpoint. Concept mapping depicts the children's viewpoint. Basically, the map consists of a network of nodes and lines. The nodes show concepts, ideas, or items of information the children remember about the subject or lesson they are mapping; the lines show connections the children perceive between ideas. Maps may be the work of individuals as in Figure 7-1 (page 90), or small groups as in Figure 7-2 (page 91). In either case, the teacher may simply observe or serve as a facilitator—asking questions, commenting, receiving, illustrating, and so forth.

Number Logs

Like mapping, logging numbers emphasizes the children's point of view; unlike the spatial representation of mapping, however, logging is chronological. A log may be continuous, listing numbers as children encounter them throughout the day or periodic, with entries for specific times or intervals. Keeping the numbers log develops observational skills as well as an awareness of numbers in everyday life. Figure 7-3 on page 92 shows the beginning of a continuous log; observations have been made at random but marked with time and place.

Numbers, Math, and Art

As a young algebra student, I remember being asked to grade my own homework assignments. All of us in the class were scrupulously honest about marking errors, but sometimes the number missed was embarrassing; therefore, we would disguise

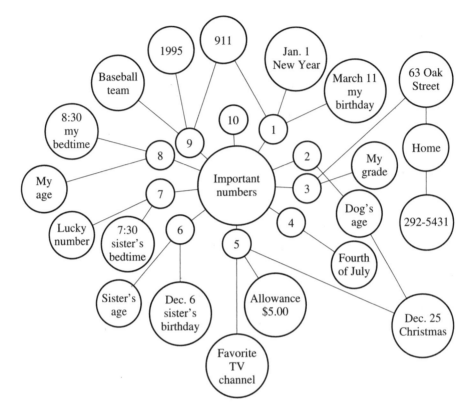

FIGURE 7-1   Third-Grader's Map of Important Numbers

it with a drawing. That began a numbers–art contest that continued to the end of the school year.

Using numbers and geometric figures in designs and drawings promotes familiarity with the visual tools of math, introduces spatial problems such as matching angles in isosceles triangles, and blurs artificial distinctions between math and other creative activities. Is math a creative activity? Of course. Like all problem-solving activities, mathematics results in constructs or thought structures that are in fact creative works. Moreover, mathematical principles underlie the execution of much fine art, including painting, sculpture, music, and dance. Ask children to discover the numbers in a music measure or dance and the math in a sculpture or cubist drawing. Then have them incorporate their discoveries in creations of their own. The result will be hands-on math/art activities that respond directly to the children's perceptions of reality and at the same time demonstrate to them the tangible and immediate potential for using mathematical ideas in the real world.

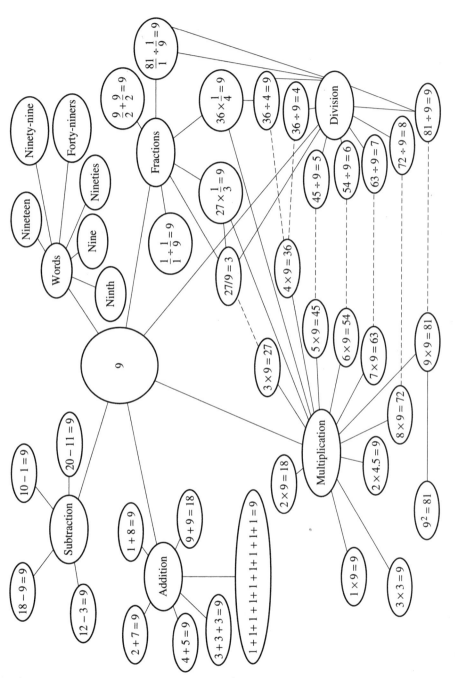

FIGURE 7-2 Fifth-Graders' Map of 9

FIGURE 7-3   Fourth-Grader's Numbers Log

When	*Where*	*Numbers*
7:12	home	1 bowl mush; 1 glass milk; TV on Channel 7; 37° outside
7:35	bus	22 on bus—17 girls, 5 boys, 9 blocks to school; bus driver, about age of grandfather, 50; turn right on Fourth Street, left on Third
8:05	school	Room 10B; 30 kids, 20 girls, 10 boys; two pieces of chalk; two doors to room; one teacher, one teacher's helper; turn in money for selling 15 candy bars at $1.00, $15.00; no commission; TV on at 5
10:30	PE room	50 yard dash; 15 minutes of slow jogging; 15 minutes of basketball; no girls; 12 boys; relays on the 50 yard dash; Team 3 beats Team 1, 2 and 4

Using Numbers and Math to Interpret the Real World

When children discover numbers in the world around them, those numbers have meaning because the world has meaning. The same principle applies when we use numbers or math concepts to interpret that world. Introduce weights and measurements in a textbook table, and they are abstract ideas. Weigh and measure each member of the class, the teacher, and the class gerbil, and kilograms, grams, pounds, ounces, meters, centimeters, feet, and inches have meaning.

Teaching math with reality-based activities is a three-step process:

1. Link real numbers to the children's real world.
2. Explore the relationship between the two.
3. Apply concepts to solve problems.

The three stages actually mirror the learning process—recognizing, understanding, and using; they ensure that the activities are meaningful in the children's own terms and that they go beyond simply illustrating concepts to teaching skills for interpreting the world. For example, a preschool teacher who uses cookies to demonstrate numbers in counting might catch the children's interest because they probably like cookies. But if he presents a plate of cookies and a problem—Do we have enough cookies for everyone in the class?—he has created a meaningful counting activity with meaningful consequences for each child—eating or not eating a cookie.

Counting activities, of course, need not be limited to preschoolers. *How many, how much,* and *how often* are key questions for statisticians at all levels. Moreover, counting need not be limited to things. Counting behaviors and events can help broaden children's understanding of numbers concepts and also develop observation skills and attention spans. In the early grades, counting for totals can help students understand their physical environment—the number of houses on their block or street, the number of apartments in their building, and the relationship of their house or apartment number to that total; the number of swings and the number of children on the playground and the resulting need to take turns; slices of cake and number of helpings; and so forth. In the later elementary grades, activities can begin with counting, then move on to finding frequencies or averages—that is, using basic operations to interpret data. For example, sixth-graders might start by counting their calorie consumption for a period of one or two weeks, then use division to find the daily average and multiplication to estimate monthly or yearly consumption.

While discovery exercises will reveal different numbers interests for different classes, some real-world ties that work for many elementary-level children are *time, distance,* and *speed.* (Games, another favorite number experience, will be discussed in Chapter 8.)

Time

How old are you? What time is it? How long until Christmas? Until your birthday? All of these questions can serve as starting points for sequenced activities that combine learning about numbers and learning about the world.

Activity #1
1. How old are you? (Items a–b, ages 6–7; Items a–e, ages 7–11)

   a. in years?
   b. in months?
   c. in weeks?
   d. in days?
   e. in hours?

2. How old is each member of your family? (Items a–b, ages 6–7; Items a–e, ages 7–11)

   a. in years?
   b. in months?
   c. in weeks?
   d. in days?
   e. in hours?

3. What is your date of birth (month, day, year)?
4. What is the date of birth (month, day, year) for each member of your family?
5. How old will you be in 5 years? In 10 years? In 20 years?

6. How old will each member of your family be in 5 years? In 10 years? In 20 years?
7. If you had been born a year earlier, how old would you be now? Two years earlier? Five years earlier? Ten years earlier?
8. If you had been born a year later, what would be your date of birth (month, day, year)? Two years later? Five years later? Ten years later?

Activity #2: What time is it? (Ages 10–11)
Give a small group a globe marked with time zones and a problem: Plan a video conference linking Tokyo, London, New York, Honolulu, Los Angeles, and Melbourne.

1. What will be the best time for the conference?
2. What will be the time in each of those cities?
3. If the conference includes a meal, what meal will participants be eating in each city?

Activity #3: How long until Christmas? (Ages 8–9)
1. Find today's date on a calendar.
2. Find Christmas on the same calender.
3. Count the months, weeks, and days until Christmas.
4. Compute the hours, minutes, and seconds until Christmas.
5. Does it seem like a long time or a short time? Why?
6. Make a week-by-week schedule of things to do before Christmas. (Ask your teacher and family for help with dates and items.)
7. If you went to sleep and slept until the year 2010, how many Christmases would you miss?
8. If you give one Christmas present a year to each member of your family, each relative, and each friend, how many presents will you give by the year 2000?
9. If 10 people give you a present each year, how many thank-yous will you have written by the year 2003? 2010? 2023?

In each activity the topic affects children's worlds directly, the process involves interacting with real-world facts, and the results are not simply answers to math problems but useful strategies and skills for interacting with their worlds. Other "time" activities that work at the elementary level include telling time with digital and round-face clocks for the early grades and with a class-made sundial for the upper grades; what-if exercises like those in Activity #1 (What if today were 50 years in the past or in the future? What if the earth revolved in 12 or 48 hours instead of 24? What if a year had 24 months instead of 12?); and timed observations (the number and frequency of cars at an intersection, of coughs or laughs or blinks; the time it takes to eat an ice cream cone, a bowl of oatmeal, a popsicle, etc.).

Distance

Exploring the concept of distance introduces measurements of space but also builds on time studies. Generally, when children ask how far it is to school or the mall or a vacation cabin, they want measurements, not just of space but of the time it takes to get there. We can begin orienting children to the relationship between the two concepts by linking them in our activities. Initially, I like to let children find their own measures before I introduce the standard systems.

Activity #4: How far is it? (Items 1–3, age 7: items 1–4, ages 8–9; items 1–5, ages 10–11)

1. How many steps from your chair to the classroom door? To the water fountain? To the restroom? To the fire escape?
2. How long in seconds does it take you to get from your chair to each of those places if you count to 3 before each step? If you don't count at all?
3. Compare your answers to your classmates' answers. How are they alike? How are they different?
4. Use a measuring stick or tape to find the number of meters and centimeters or feet and inches in each of the distances in item one.
5. How many centimeters or inches were you moving per second when you timed yourself?

Walking a mile or a kilometer, drawing maps to scale, or measuring a quarter of a mile in string—each of these activities not only introduces the concepts of distance and measurement but also makes them tangible—something that can be experienced physically and remembered with vivid images. Math activities about distance should be integrated with geography and science lessons, with clear applications to show how math helps us understand and interact with the physical world.

Speed

Time and distance activities prepare children to understand the concept of speed; nevertheless, their readiness is by and large at the concrete rather than at the abstract level. That is, children are ready to experience speed or speeds rather than absorb a formula such as:

$$speed = distance/time$$

How fast (or slow) are we going? How fast (or slow) can we go? How fast (or slow) should we go? These are questions that call for doing before calculating and, of course, understanding before applying.

Activity #5: How fast (or slow) are we going? (Ages 9–10)

Measure a distance such as 50 meters on the playground. Then give each small group of students a stopwatch. Have them appoint a record keeper or rotate record keeping as each student runs and walks the distance. Back in the classroom, have students compute and graph individual speeds, determine the average for the group, and compare it with other groups' averages.

Activity #6: How fast (or slow) should we go? (Ages 7–8)
1. Make a map of the speed signs on the streets and in the parking lots around your school.
2. Which signs call for the slowest speeds? Which call for the fastest speeds?
3. What do the speeds mean?
4. Explain the reasons for the different speeds.

Activity #7: How fast (or slow) can we go. (Age 11)
1. Use a road map to plan an automobile trip from Seattle, Washington, to Miami, Florida, and back.
2. How many miles will the trip be?
3. How long will it take you to make the trip if you travel an average of 55 miles per hour, six hours a day? 50 miles per hour, eight hours a day? 45 miles per hour, 10 hours a day?
4. Would it be possible to make the entire trip in a week? In 10 days? Why or why not?

Real Math and Math Anxiety

Tying math activities to children's worlds does more than combat math anxiety. Children who see math as real in their own terms are more likely to be confident— to feel in control of the activities and through them in control of the concepts. Confidence negates anxiety; it also reverses anxiety's effects, such as lack of interest, attention, or motivation.

Teachers sometimes tell me, "Hands-on activities work, but who has time for them? I have a syllabus to get through." My immediate response is a comment and question. The standard curriculum requires teachers to go through the same material year after year in grade after grade. Wouldn't it save time to replace many skim-through lessons with one thorough learning experience?

Questions for Thought and Discussion

1. How might adults' and children's realities differ? How might their perceptions of numbers mirror these differences?
2. What does it mean when we say that numbers are real? Can numbers be unreal?
3. Which business-math subjects should be taught in elementary school? Which should not be taught?
4. What kinds of manipulatives work in math activities? What kinds do not work? Why?

Activities

1. Take your blood pressure at regular intervals during the day. Record the results over a three-week period. Compute the arithmetic averages by day and by week. Graph your data with the days on the horizontal axis and the blood pressure readings on the vertical anxis.
2. Record the calories you consume, item by item and day by day, during a typical two- week period. Compute averages, and graph the results.
3. Develop a chart of "real" math activities, suitable for various elementary levels. Include children's ages, concepts to be learned, skills to be developed, materials needed, and estimates of time for completion.

Annotated List of Readings

Roberts, A. Wayne, and Dale E. Varberg. *Faces of Mathematics.* New York: Harper & Row, 1982. 2nd ed. *Readable introduction to the real number system. Illustrates problem-solving situaions.*

Ruedy, Elisabeth, and Sue Nirenberg. *Where Do I Put the Decimal Point? How to Conquer Math Anxiety and Increase Your Facility with Numbers.* New York: Henry Holt, 1990. *Delightful treatment of real numbers in the context of conquering math anxiety. Works through applied-to-real-life problems in a nonthreatening way.*

8

Teaching Math Through Play

Sometimes it is not enough to make math real. We need to make math fun.

Is that possible? Some people would say no: "If you're having fun, you're not doing math; and if you're doing math, you're not having fun." Others would say it is neither possible nor desirable: "Serious math learning calls for disciplined, consistent, diligent thinking—not fun and games." One math teacher told me, "I'm not a clown, and this class is not a circus. We do not play games here."

These attitudes, of course, take us back to the distress that underlies math anxiety. Grim teaching and grim subject matter evoke grim responses. If a subject is too important and too serious to laugh about, learning becomes a "necessary evil"; we must "grin and bear it," "keep a stiff upper lip," "bite the bullet," "take our medicine"—all the get-down-to-business clichés adults use to get through an unpleasant task. Stresses, then, conflict; pressure to learn combats the pressure not to learn, resulting in distress and anxiety and diminished rather than increased learning capacity.

In a sense, the anomaly here is not learning math through play, but learning anything without play. Play is nature's school. When bobcat kittens stalk and pounce or bear cubs roll and tumble, they are learning survival skills. Learning is active, exuberant, joyous—the antithesis, in fact, of the traditional, straight-rows, eyes-forward, no-talking classroom.

Some teachers would argue that we are talking apples and oranges. Perhaps. The animals are learning physical skills; the children are learning mental skills. But the distinction may be less one of kind than of degree. A difference in subject matter may affect learning materials but not the learning process. Learning to leap distances and learning to measure distances both require paying attention, grasping purpose and method, coordinating a number of different variables simultaneously, and practicing perfect technique.

Video and computer games, board games like Monopoly, geometric puzzles, *Mathnet* on PBS—all provide useful math play and can even serve as homework assignments. However, math play in the classroom calls for a tighter focus on specific learning goals and an emphasis on concepts rather than competition. Often the most effective activities are teacher-made rather than ready-made because, instead of fitting students to the activities, teachers will fit play to the students' abilities and needs.

Some general guidelines for math play in the classroom follow:

1. Design the activity lesson plan with specific learning goals and objectives.
2. Create activities primarily for groups rather than individuals because working together is both a learning tool and a learning goal.
3. Emphasize understanding rather than winning.
4. Emphasize doing rather than observing.
5. Emphasize everyone-can rather than only-a-few-can.
6. Make the activity itself rather than its outcome a reward.

Math play, such as math puzzles and math games, might serve as the "spoonful of sugar" introducing a more traditional math lesson, or might constitute the lesson itself. Either way, play provides a context for learning and gives it meaning. Many teachers find "doing for fun" a much better motivator than doing to understand the stock market or the family budget or even space travel and propulsion systems.

Math Games

"Let's play a game!" How many times have those words ended a bout of the mulligrubs or softened a blow or reversed a tantrum? Many marketed games include some type of math, and an hour of play can be a more productive homework assignment than repetitive exercises or tortuously worded problems.

But there is a place for games in the classroom as well. We mentioned in Chapter 5 the need to rehearse or repeat information as part of the learning process. Couch rehearsal in recitations, reviews, and repetitive exercises, and the result is drudgery. Make rehearsal part of a game, and the result is fun.

Math games provide practice for skills, a way to repeat while minimizing the boredom factor, and an opportunity to experiment with problem-solving strategies. While winnng or losing is implicit in the game idea, teachers can deemphasize competition and emphasize individual achievement by having children keep logs of their scores and work for a personal best.

Replacing drill with games. Any drill topic—addition, subtraction, multiplication tables, and so forth—can be made into a game. Remember flash cards? For years, well-meaning teachers used them in drills that intimidated or bored generations of students. But a set of flash cards makes a good card game, or game cards can easily be drawn on 3 × 5 cards. Dice also work well for math games. Rolling a pair automatically creates an addition problem, or you can multiply the numbers, subtract the smaller from the larger or the larger from the smaller, divide and reduce for fractions, add and multiply for squares. Students can play in teams with a math "whiz" as leader or in groups with similar achievement records to give everyone a level playing field.

Flash Card Draw

3–5 players.
Age and grade level matched to difficulty of the cards.

Game Rules
1. Place flash cards on table with answer side down.
2. Each player draws three cards and holds them so that other players see the problem but not the answers.
3. Play begins with the player whose birthdate is the highest number.
4. That player selects problems to solve from the cards in other players' hands. Each time the player correctly solves a problem, he or she collects the card and places it in the solved stack (individual if students are playing to win, group if they are playing to beat the clock). The player's turn continues until she or he misses an answer, draws another card from the center stack, and passes play to his or her right.
5. Play continues until all the cards in the center stack are gone, or the time allotted for play is over.
6. If the students are playing against the clock, they record the number of cards in the solved stack and try to increase the number each time they play. If they are playing to win, they add the number of cards in their own solved stacks. The student with the highest number wins the game.

Match and Draw

3–5 players.
Age and grade level matched to difficulty of problems.

Materials: Two sets of 3 × 5 cards, one set with problems (addition, subtraction, multiplication, division, fractions, decimals, or a mixture of two or more types) and one set with answers.

Game Rules
1. Answer and problem cards are placed face down in two stacks at the center of table.
2. Each player draws three problem cards and three answer cards.
3. Play begins with the student whose name comes last in the alphabet.
4. The player tries to match problems with answers in his or her hand. If an answer matches a problem, the player says "match" and lays the cards down. The players check the match. If it is correct, the player leaves the matched cards on the table and draws from each stack on the table, continuing play until he or she can no longer make a match.
5. Players may draw from the center stacks at two different times:
   a. when they make a match,
   b. when they complete their turns.
6. Play moves from left to right.
7. Play continues until all the cards in the center stack are gone or the time alloted for play is over.
8. The player with the most matched sets wins the game.

Variation: Players may call on each other for specific problem or answer cards. If the call is answered correctly, the player's turn continues; if the call is answered incorrectly, the player's turn ends.

Roll and Draw

3–5 players.
Grades 4–5.

Materials: 2 dice and a set of 60 cards—10 marked *add;* 10, *subtract;* 25, *multiply;* and 15, *divide*. Pencils and score cards for each player.

Game Rules
1. The player whose name has the most letters starts the game.
2. The player rolls the dice and draws a card. If the card says "multiply," the player multiplies the dice numbers. If it says "divide," the player divides the larger number by the smaller number, and so forth.
3. A correct answer is the player's score for that roll. The other players may use a calculator to check answers.
4. The player's turn continues until he or she makes an error or the total score for that turn exceeds 100.
5. The player then returns all cards face down to the bottom of the deck, and gives the dice to the player on the right.
6. Play continues for a specified period or until one player's score tops 1,000.

Variations:
  a. Increase the number of dice to four and use totals from each set for the operations.
  b. Add double-operations cards to the stack.
  c. Increase the top score to 5,000 or 10,000.

How Many Ways Can You ... ?

Groups of 2 or 3
All grades (depending on the task)

Tasks:
  1. How many ways can you cut a 4″ × 7″ cake so that 14 people can have equal-sized pieces?
  2. How many ways can you add 40 + 4 + 100 + 9 + 2 + 17 + 32?
  3. How many ways can you multiply 10 times 10 times 22 times 44?
  4. How many ways can you find the area of a 90 degree triangle when the shorter sides are 4 centimeters and 7 centimeters?
  5. How many ways can you find to count the number of seats in a school auditorium if there are 30 rows, a center aisle, and 15 seats in each row on both sides of the aisle?
  6. How many ways can you work the following problems:

$$2 + 2 + 2 + 2 - 2 - 2 - 2 - 2 =$$

$$10 \times 10 \times 10 \times 10 \times 4 - 4 =$$

$$\frac{1}{2} + \frac{1}{2} + \frac{1}{2} + \frac{1}{2} - \frac{1}{2} - \frac{1}{2} - \frac{1}{2} - \frac{1}{2} =$$

$$\frac{1}{2} \times \frac{1}{2} \times \frac{1}{2} \times \frac{1}{2} \div \frac{1}{2} \div \frac{1}{2} \div \frac{1}{2} =$$

$$100 \div .10 \times .001 \times 100 \div 10 =$$

  7. How many ways can you divide a dollar so that you and three friends have equal amounts?
  8. How many ways can you find the area of a wall that is 8 feet high and 12 feet long and has a 3-by-6-foot door in the middle?
  9. How many ways can you find to add, subtract, multiply, and divide?

Exploring problem-solving strategies with games. A major problem with most standard curricula is rigidity: to do this type of exercise, follow only these steps; to get the right answer, follow exclusively this procedure. We should not blame this rigidity on teachers or teaching materials. Because education as a whole follows a linear path, with emphasis on evaluation and learning outcomes, students themselves and their parents will insist that teachers present the "right" or "quickest" or "best" way to solve math problems. Parents often will complain if their children are allowed to experiment with accepted procedures, such as adding or multiplying multidigit numbers beginning with the right-hand column. Beginning at the left and moving to the right may not be as efficient, but it does present a different perspective; moreover, children who have tried adding both ways may have a better grasp of the process and be able to estimate answers more accurately.

Adding from the Left	*Adding from the Right*
	11
119	119
$+\ \ 82$	$+\ \ 82$
100	201
90	
11	
201	

Multiplying from the Left	*Multiplying from the Right*
29	29
$\times\ 29$	$\times\ 29$
400	261
180	58
180	841
81	
841	

Because games are play—outside the standard curriculum with its standard objectives and standard expectations—they give children the freedom to experiment. In fact, experimenting with different ways to solve math problems makes an effective math game.

A game may consist of one or more tasks. The objective is to invent as many ways as possible to solve each. The teacher might challenge teams to exceed a specific number or offer a special reward for any team that develops an original but workable strategy for solving a problem.

Math Puzzles

The how-many-ways game could also be a variety of math puzzle because, unlike most games, it explores unknowns instead of knowns. Math puzzles are numbers mysteries. The mystery might be visual; it might be spatial; it might be mathematical. Remember Rubik's cube and its dozens of clones and mutations, such as the Impossiball? Those were geometric puzzles designed primarily for teenagers and adults, but often elementary-level children succeeded in solving them. Why? The patterns underlying the solutions and the strategies needed to work the puzzles fell within children's conceptual abilities. In addition, whereas adults tended to become stuck, repeating the same unsuccessful strategies, the children were more flexible, ready to abandon what did not work and quicker to recognize what worked.

Picture Puzzles

These are puzzles that children in the early grades can make for themselves. They can start with a math poster or math art, such as a numbers collage; glue it to light posterboard; then cut the sheet into squiggly puzzle pieces. Fitting the pieces together again presents numbers in a different perspective and even exercises children's grasp of concepts since it requires them to infer from contexts what is missing or what comes next.

Cloze Procedure Puzzles

Borrowed from reading and comprehension exercises, these puzzles are related to the picture puzzles. Children fill in the gaps with numbers, working either from the beginning to the ending of the story or, if the conclusion is provided, from the ending to the beginning. Again, they develop a different perspective on numbers as well as skill in inferring from contexts.

Cloze Puzzle #1

At ____ o'clock in the morning, ____ children wake up and get ready for school. They each eat ____ egg, ____ slice of toast, and ____ of a grapefruit. They put on ____ socks, ____ shoes, ____ pair of pants, and ____ shirt. They pack ____ books in their book bags and take ____ for lunch in the cafeteria. By ____ they are on the bus riding with ____ other students to the school, ____ blocks away.

Cloze Puzzle #2

The ____ grade class is collecting money for the homeless. Susie collected ____ from shoppers at the mall. Hans went door to door in his neighborhood and got ____. Albert, Teresa, and Ricardo each collected ____ while their fathers shopped at the super market. Six other children brought in ____ each, and ten gave ____ each. The teacher added ____ or a total of $56.32.

Words in Numbers Puzzles

Children are intrigued by number–word homophones—numbers and words or syllables that sound alike but mean different things. Unraveling a jumble of homophones provides a lesson in the meaning of words as well as the meaning of numbers. Children first write out a translation of the jumble, then perform any operations asked for with the numbers.

Jumble #1

Too police officers of 10 work 2gether 4 safety. If too officers are assigned 2 ate square blocks, how many officers are needed 4 a downtown area of foreteaate square blocks?

Jumble #2

2 cut a cake measuring ate inches by ate inches in ate pieces, first cut it in2 equal halves, then in for equal pieces, then in ate equal pieces. 2 find the size 4 each piece, divide the area of the cake by ate. Each piece will be too inches wide and for inches long.

Cross-Number Puzzles

Books are filled with this type of puzzle, but teachers can make them easily. Cross-number puzzles dress up exercises and practice that might otherwise seem repetitive or boring. Figure 8-1 on page 106 shows a cross-number puzzle.

Children catch on quickly to the duplication of effort here but can be asked to work both the down and the across problems to double check their answers. Advanced students can start with the numbers filled in and work backwards to create the problems.

Figure 8-2 on page 106 is another cross-number puzzle with blanks by the numbers for clues. Using the exact answers from Puzzle #1, Figure 8-2 represents a variation of Puzzle #1.

Another variation calls for a mixture of clues and puzzle numbers. Students fill in whatever has been left blank. Figure 8-3 on page 107 shows a cross-number puzzle with mixed operations.

Down:

1. 21 × 21
2. 15 × 15
3. 23 × 22
4. 3 × 104
5. 15 × 17
6. 17 × 18
7. 16 × 14
8. 9 × 23
9. 5 × 29

Across:

1. 25 × 17
2. 7 × 60
3. 3 × 52
4. 19 × 17
5. 10 × 25
6. 28 × 27
7. 13 × 17
8. 17 × 12
9. 29 × 19

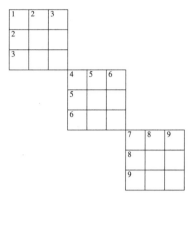

FIGURE 8-1   Puzzle #1—Multiplication

Down:

1.
2.
3.
4.
5.
6.
7.
8.
9.

Across:

1.
2.
3.
4.
5.
6.
7.
8.
9.

1 4	2 2	3 5
2 4	2	0
3 1	5	6

4 3	5 2	6 3
5 2	5	0
6 7	5	6

7 2	8 2	9 1
8 2	0	4
9 4	7	5

FIGURE 8-2   Variation of Puzzle #1

Down:

1. $4610 - 20 =$
2. $474 \times 18 =$
3. $200 \times 21 =$
4. $15784 \div 2 =$
5. $2020 - 999 =$
6. $1450 + 607 =$
7. $35 \times 45 =$
8. $27 \times 51 =$
9. $2352 \div 2 =$
10. $37 \times 37 =$
11. $36 \times 39 =$
12. $10610 \div 2 =$

Across:

1. $22 \times 22 =$
2. $23 \times 24 =$
3. $990 - 60 =$
4. $300 - 280 =$
5. $8 \times 89 =$
6. $40 \times 20 =$
7. $25 \times 37 =$
8. $7 \times 31 =$
9. $222 \div 22 =$
10. $9 \times 59 =$
11. $111 \times 7 =$
12. $8 \times 72 =$
13. $5 \times 23 =$
14. $7 \times 49 =$
15. $24 \times 25 =$
16. $35 \times 27 =$

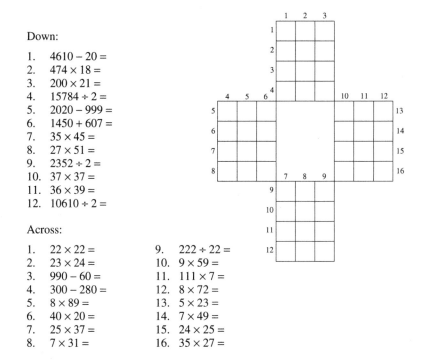

FIGURE 8-3   Math Puzzle #2, Mixed Operations

What-Comes-Next Puzzles

These puzzles either ask children to recognize a pattern and infer the next logical component or let children create their own systems for working with groups of numbers. Seriation puzzles can use images or numbers. In each of the sets of puzzles in Figure 8-4 on page 108, the children should continue the series through the entire set.

Continuing a series is open ended in the sense that the puzzle never comes to an end, but the process is prescribed and therefore restricted. Puzzles that let the children decide which operations to use and when to use them are more truly open ended. Because there is no trick solution and no single correct answer, the puzzles call for original rather than imitative problem solving. Children can work alone or in groups, but either way it helps to talk out the process. Figure 8-5 on page 109 presents several sets of informal math series.

**What-Comes-Next Puzzles for the Early Grades
(Kindergarten–Early Second Grade)**

1. ⃝⃝ ⃝⃝⃝ ⃝⃝⃝⃝ ⃝⃝⃝⃝⃝ _____

2. ∿ ∿∿ ∿∿∿ ∿∿∿∿ _____

3. ⃝⃝□ ⃝⃝⃝⃝□□ ⃝⃝⃝⃝⃝⃝□□□□ _____

4. △△△△ △△△ △△ _____

5. ⃝△⃝ ⃝△⃝△ ⃝△⃝△⃝ _____

**What-Comes-Next Puzzles for the Middle Grades
(Late Second Grade–Early Fourth Grade)**

1.	2	4	6	8	10	12	____
2.	1	3	5	7	9	11	____
3.	5	10	15	20	25	30	____
4.	21	22	24	25	27	28	____
5.	7	14	21	28	35	42	____

**What-Comes-Next Puzzles for the Upper Grades
(Late Fourth Grade–Early Sixth Grade)**

1.	3	7	11	15	19		____
2.	4	6	9	13.5		20.25	____
3.	2×4		4×16		16×256		____
4.	4	10	22	46	____		
5.	19	10	6	4	____		

FIGURE 8-4   What-Comes-Next Puzzles

FIGURE 8-5　Math Chains

Puzzle A: The Chain

Chain the numbers together by adding, subtracting, multiplying, or dividing adjacent pairs. Do not use the same operation twice in a row. Do use each operation at least once.

Example:　2　1　3　4　5　6
2 + 1 = 3, 3/3 = 1, 1 × 4 = 4, 4 + 5 = 9, 9 − 6 = 3

1.　7　　2　　8　　4　　2　　9
2.　11　12　8　　8　　9　　6
3.　1　　3　　5　　7　　9　　11

Puzzle B: How High?

Add, subtract, multiply, or divide the numbers in a chain of calculations for the highest possible total. Use each operation at least once. Work with the numbers in any order, but write out all calculations.

Example:　2　3　4　5　1
5 × 4 = 20, 20 − 2 = 18, 18 ÷ 1 = 18, 18 + 3 = 21

1.　7　　1　　3　　8　　6
2.　9　　9　　9　　9　　9
3.　2　　6　　5　　10　4

Variation: Compute for the lowest possible total.

Math Play in the Kitchen

Children learn more practical math in the kitchen than in many classrooms. Measuring cups and spoons not only teach measurements, but also fractions—1/2 cup, 1/4 cup, 1/3 cup, 2/4 cup, 1/8 teaspoon, 1/4 teaspoon, 1/2 teaspoon. And because cooking is a hands-on activity, the amount can be seen, touched, and manipulated. Children like the different textures of common kitchen ingredients—sugar, corn meal, flour, oats, oils, and syrups—and they are inexpensive enough that we can use them freely in "show rather than tell" exercises. Tell children that three teaspoons make one tablespoon, and they may or may not remember. Let them discover the fact by spooning teaspoons full of sugar into a tablespoon, and they will never forget.

The kitchen offers math lessons for all levels. Preschoolers can cut cookie dough in geometric shapes. Kindergartners can count chocolate drops, M&M's, and raisins to put in each cookie. First- and second-graders can follow directions to measure ingredients; third- and fourth-graders can follow a recipe, measure ingredients and mix them; and fifth- and sixth-graders can make adjustment for altitude or translate a recipe with metric measurements into cups, tablespoons, and teaspoons.

Cooking play also offers nonthreatening lessons in accountability. Make a mistake in measurements, and the result may be inedible. Measure correctly, and the result is an immediate, tangible reward.

Math Play Out of Doors and Out of the Classroom

For years math has been tarred and feathered with the image of an indoors, quiet-room activity. But *real* math belongs everywhere—in the shop, out of doors, on the basketball court, in the shotput ring, in the skating rink. One danger of tying math activities to calculators and computers is that the how of doing math is confused with the reality of what math is; in other words, math is not solely the province of computer or calculator technology. Because computers and calculators are tools for calculation, the association between them and doing math is expected. However, because mathematics is everywhere in our varied environments; because it exists across time from the moment we get up at a certain time to the moment we call it quits for the day; because it plays a dominant role in our lives, the reality of math is far greater than any single technology. Another danger in linking math activities to calculators and computers is limiting their mobility. Mental math skills and scratch calculations can go anywhere. As a youngster, I used a stick on dirt and chalk on a sidewalk to keep score or make calculations. In spite of my solar pocket calculator, I still tend to cover café napkins, torn envelopes picked up in the park, or paper towels from public restrooms with figures and calculations that cannot wait until I get back to my desk or computer.

Being a Surveyor

Some of our favorite heroes like George Washington and Daniel Boone were surveyors. They used math to measure their world and to describe and define their environment. Assign students to make a survey map of their home or school. With a measuring tape or stick, they can find out the size of their house or apartment building or school. Then they can measure the area around it, including the yard or playground. They should carefully note each structure (such as garages, toolsheds, or fences); each piece of playground equipment; and each tree, shrub, or flowerbed and place them accurately on the map.

To make an accurate map, they will need to work to scale—so many inches or centimeters to so many feet or meters.

Following the Trails

Prepare several sets of numerical clues to guide students along different trails to specific locations in your school building or campus. One trail might lead to the library, another to the cafeteria, and another around the building and back to the classroom. Clues can include specific measures (20′ south, 14′ west), compass headings, visual clues such as room or street numbers, and object counts or descriptions (3 trees, right angle in sidewalk, triangular street sign).

Variations in the clues can cause trails to diverge or converge. Students should work in small groups. You might put a prize or a treat at the end of each trail, or have the scouts bring a token back to the classroom to collect a reward.

Keeping Score/Finding Percentages

Commandeer the basketball courts on the playground for a session of throwing hoops. Divide the class into small groups—enough to match the number of hoops. Then have students throw baskets, keeping track of the total number of throws and the total number of baskets. Have each person compute his or her percentage accuracy; then have each group calculate their percentage accuracy. Additionally, you could have them earn extra points as the distance from the basket increases. You could weight distance by some factor before taking your averages.

Questions for Thought and Discussion

1. How many games that you have played involve math? What skills could playing those games develop?
2. Do you like puzzles? Are you good at solving them? Why or why not?
3. In what ways might learning by play differ from learning by traditional methods? What are the advantages? What are the disadvantages?
4. How do you think parents might react to games as math homework?

Activities

1. Create a math game to develop a specific skill or group of skills. Focus the game carefully for age group and educational activities. If possible, test the game with the target group as well as several other groups for comparison.
2. Translate a standard arithmetic exercise into a math puzzle. Give the exercise and the puzzle to different groups of students. Do the groups perform equally well?
3. Start a math-play scrapbook to serve as an activities resource book. Include games you and others have made, puzzles from game books and newspapers, activity sheets collected from other teachers, and ideas for future development.

Annotated List of Readings

Ekeland, Ivar. *The Broken Dice,* trans. Carol Volk. Chicago: University of Chicago Press, 1991. *Mathematical tales of chance. Mixes mathematics and mythology.*

Flansburg, Scott, with Victoria Hay. *Math Magic.* New York: William Morrow, 1993. *Antidote for life-long math phobias. Approaches everyday math problems and math learning as fun, easy activities accessible to everyone.*

9

Teaching Math through Reading and Writing

Too often adults (including teachers) identify themselves as "word people" or "numbers people." The dichotomy underscores the either–or thinking that tries to legitimate learning anxieties by tying them to learning preferences or learning abilities. Adults may *say*, "I don't *do* math because I'm a word person" or "Reading and writing are not my thing because I'm a numbers person." But they *mean,* "I avoid math because I feel my skills are inadequate, but I read and write well" or "My language skills are poor, but I'm good at computations."

It is human nature, of course, to like what we are good at; it is also human nature to make excuses for our inadequacies. In this case, however, the excuse hides a complex structure of learning and attitudinal problems—some related to individual learning strategies, some related to educational systems. Moreover, it reinforces a way of thinking that handicaps math learning by restricting the ways in which children interact with knowledge. I will discuss stereotyping as a dimension of these problems in Chapter 11; in this chapter I want to propose at least a partial solution: using reading and writing to teach mathematics.

Children enter school with sophisticated language skills. Traditional mathematics instruction takes little advantage of these "ordinary" language skills, emphasizing instead the acquisition and use of special mathematical language. The method is comparable to instructing bilingual students in a second, imperfectly understood language: some of the content blurs in translation.

Reading and writing about mathematics in ordinary language enable children to work from the familiar to the unfamiliar. More importantly, they can draw on ordinary language's enormous cognitive resources to help them interact with, structure, and assimilate concepts. Consider, for example, two versions of the same lesson: how to find the area of a triangle.

Version A

Explanation: To find the area of a triangle, use the formula: $A = 1/2\ bh$, where A = area in square units, b = base, and h = height.

Problem: If $b = 6$ cm and $h = 8$ cm, what is the area of the triangle?

Solution: $1/2 \times 6$ cm $\times 8$ cm $= 48/2 = 24$ cm^2

Version B

Explanation: You have already learned how to use length and width to find the distance around, or the perimeter, of rectangles. You also know how to use length and width to find the amount of space inside, or the area of rectangles. You can use the same figures (with different names) to find the area of this triangle:

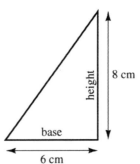

If the triangle were part of a rectangle whose length and width were the same as the triangle's height and base, how would you find the area of the rectangle?

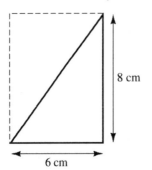
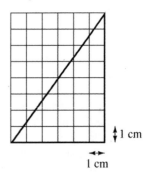

You could divide the space into centimeters and count the number of square centimeters. Or you could multiply the number of centimeters in the width by the number of centimeters in the length.

$$6 \text{ cm} \times 8 \text{ cm} = 48 \text{ cm}^2$$

If the triangle is half the size of the rectangle, how would you find the triangle's area? You could count and add the number of square centimeters (whole and part) in the triangle half of the drawing above. Or you could multiply the base of the triangle by the height and divide by 2.

$$\frac{6 \text{ cm} \times 8 \text{ cm}}{2} = 24 \text{ cm}^2$$

Concept: If the formula for finding the area of a rectangle is $A = lw$, what formula can you make for finding the area of a triangle? Explain the formula in your own words.

Answer:
$$A = \frac{bh}{2}$$

To find the area of a triangle, you first find the area of a rectangle, then divide that number in half.

Problems: Find the area of these triangles:

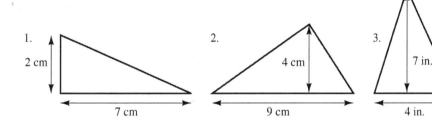

1. 2 cm   7 cm

2. 4 cm   9 cm

3. 7 in.   4 in.

Solutions:

1. $\dfrac{2 \text{ cm} \times 7 \text{ cm}}{2} = \dfrac{14}{2} = 7 \text{ cm}^2$

2. $\dfrac{4 \text{ cm} \times 9 \text{ cm}}{2} = \dfrac{36}{2} = 18 \text{ cm}^2$

3. $\dfrac{7 \text{ in} \times 4 \text{ in.}}{2} = \dfrac{28}{2} = 14 \text{ in.}^2$

Discussion: What else have you learned from this lesson?

Response: When we are talking about rectangles, we can use width and
              mean the short side and length to mean the long side, but
              with triangles it is better to say base and height because
              sometimes the base is shorter than the height.
              Also, it doesn't matter what units we use to measure. Area is
              still in square units like square centimeters, square inches,
              square miles, or square meters.

Discussion: How do you feel about this lesson? Was it easy, hard, impor-
                  tant, unimportant? Can you use this information in real life?

Response: This lesson was easy because I already knew how to find the
                  area of a rectangle. It might be important later on when I
                  study more geometry, but I probably won't use it much.
                  My teacher said I might need to find the area of a rectan-
                  gle to know how many square feet of carpet I should buy
                  for a floor or how much paint to cover a wall. Not many
                  walls or floors are in the shape of a triangle, although a
                  flower bed or lawn might be. I could use the area to tell
                  me how much peat moss or grass sod to buy.

Version A is written primarily in mathematical language. The explanation provides the barest facts, a formula for students to use. Students respond in the same
way, plugging numbers into the formula. The lesson emphasizes how to find the
area of a triangle, with little attention to what this means and none to why the formula works or how the information interacts with other concepts. Some students
may fill in the gaps on their own, but most will simply memorize and use the formula without really understanding what it means.

Version B, on the other hand, is what a skeptical colleague calls the "wordy"
version. It uses ordinary language to fill in or cause students to fill in the conceptual gaps. Students read and write their way through the lesson, using these basic
language skills to help them focus their thinking and integrate concepts. Most students would probably complete both versions successfully, but none could complete
Version B successfully without a thorough grasp of the concepts involved, including a conceptual framework that makes the information part of a greater whole. Version B may take longer, but children who have read and written their way through
the information are less likely to forget it, less likely to misapply or confuse it, and
less likely to require yearly rehearsals of the same material.

Reading to Learn Mathematics

Enhancing the reading component of mathematics instruction begins with reading
mathematics and continues with reading about mathematics. Certainly there has always been some reading involved in math study, but for the most part that reading

has focused on mathematical language—the symbols and idioms of lessons such as Version A above. Translating mathematics into ordinary language, as in Version B, extends the reading experience, making the information more accessible—and, for many teachers, more "teachable." It also provides an effective bridge for writing to learn mathematics, discussed later in this chapter.

Reading about mathematics might involve group reading and reading aloud as well as individual reading assignments and can include interactive story-telling; cartoons, advertisements, and articles from newspapers; and adaptations of well-known literature.

Reading Math Stories.   Children love stories, both those they read and those their teachers read aloud. Stories help children "see" concepts. They also prevent math anxiety by establishing a nonthreatening context for the lessons—that is, instead of "find the correct answer," we start with "once upon a time." Unlike the word problems abhorred by much of humanity, these math stories are complete narratives. Instead of word translations of numerals and symbols, they let a math problem or illustration grow naturally from a story line or plot.

"The Cabbage Patch" is a numbers story for the early grades. The learning goals are to prepare children who count proficiently for addition and children who can add proficiently for subtraction; the specific objectives are to discover the number of red and green cabbages eaten by the rabbits and the number sold to the market. The teacher reads the story aloud, illustrating with cutouts or chalkboard drawings.

The Cabbage Patch

At the end of a dirt road, behind a tiny house sits a cabbage patch, filled with plump, delicious cabbages. There are 10 straight rows in the patch—5 of red cabbages and 5 of green—and in each row there are 10 cabbages.

All of these plump cabbages belong to 2 children, Samantha and Jonathan, who live in the tiny house. Each day Samantha and Jonathan water the cabbages and pull the weeds around them. And they think about how they will spend all of their money when they sell the cabbages to the market.

"The manager at the market will give us 25 cents for each cabbage head," said Jonathan, "25 cents for each red cabbage head and 25 cents for each green cabbage head."

"That's 25 cents for you and 25 cents for me," said Samantha, reminding Jonathan that they were equal partners in the cabbage patch.

While Samantha and Jonathan worked, another family moved next door to their cabbage patch—a family of rabbits. With 8 hungry babies to feed, Momma and Poppa Rabbit were happy to find such plump cabbages and such a big cabbage patch. After dark, when Samantha and Jonathan were asleep inside the tiny house, the rabbits visited the cabbage patch. Momma and Poppa Rabbit each ate a large green cabbage, and the baby rabbits ate all of 2 red cabbages and part of 2 others.

When the children woke up the next morning, they saw the empty spots in their neat rows of cabbages.

"Some rabbits have been stealing our cabbages!" Jonathan yelled as he ran up and down the rows.

"They ate 2 green cabbages and 2 red cabbages and spoiled 2 more," said Samantha, who was worried about profits.

That day the children built a fence all around the cabbage patch. The fence was 5 feet tall—taller than Samantha or Jonathan and higher than any rabbit could jump.

"Just try to jump this fence, you stupid rabbits!" the children shouted toward the woods, where they suspected the rabbits were hiding.

That was a mistake. The rabbits were not stupid, but they were hungry. Soon after dark, the rabbits dug a tunnel under the fence. And because digging is hard work, Momma and Poppa Rabbit each ate one red cabbage and one green cabbage. The baby rabbits, who were growing, ate all of 4 green cabbages and part of 4 red cabbages.

What do you think happened the next morning?

Leaving the story open-ended allows the teacher to continue until half or even all of the cabbages are gone. At different points in the story, the children can stop and count or add or subtract cabbages. Then, if they continue the story with more raids on the cabbage patch and more cabbages counted, added, or subtracted, they will be in effect creating their own math problems—a critical step toward "owning" the information and empowerment.

For the upper elementary grades, math stories can present a mystery, as in "The Case of the Missing Peanuts."

The Case of the Missing Peanuts

Tomás loved peanuts. He loved peanuts so much that he ate them everywhere. He ate them on the bus going to school, on the playground during recess, in the cafeteria at lunch, on the bus going home from school, and at night in his room while he did his homework.

Tomás kept his supply of peanuts in a big round jar. Because his sister Josie also liked peanuts, Tomás taped a sign on the jar: "Private Property. Keep out! (That means *you,* Josie!!!)"

To make sure Josie did not take any of his peanuts, each morning Tomás would weigh the jar and then mark and measure the level of peanuts on the side of the jar.

One morning Tomás's peanut jar weighed 8 pounds and peanuts came all the way to the top—12 inches. Since Tomás knew the jar itself weighed 3 pounds, he decided that a full jar of peanuts must weigh 5 pounds.

That day at the mall Tomás bought a 5-pound bag of peanuts and a second identical jar. When he got home, he started to fill his new jar with the bag of peanuts, but only 1/2 of the bag would fit into the jar.
What do you think happened?

Like creating math games, creating math stories should start with specific learning goals and objectives. You can make the stories interactive by calling for students' input to extend the storyline, supply key story elements, or provide a conclusion. You can also make writing math stories part of students' writing-to-learn-math experiences (discussed later in this chapter). Collect math stories by math topic—stories about addition, multiplication, fractions, volume, area, and so forth; then duplicate individual stories as exercise sheets that children can write on. Or put the entire collection on a computer disk. Children can work with the story materials and print the results without changing the original.

Reading about Math in Literature and the Media

For years, I have collected cartoons and newspaper stories that address math topics. Predictably, since cartoonists deal primarily with human foibles and frailties, most of the cartoons are about math anxiety. However, newspaper articles cover a broader range of topics and therefore promote a wider range of learning activities. For example, I used articles about the Pentium chip's division errors to initiate discussions of long division in the math curriculum and the implications of "rounding off" remainders. Some teachers use items about the national debt or trade deficits in the study of large numbers. Others use data about earthquakes and the Richter scale in studying arithmetic and geometric progressions and use car and truck advertisements for computations involving interest rates and monthly payments.

Many teachers draw on real-world numbers for math lessons, but reading data in a news item or advertisement is a different learning experience from reading the extrapolated data in a math problem. Not only is the newspaper written in ordinary language, but it also presents a meaningful context that a math problem only assumes. Moreover, if the students themselves extract data and translate it into the math language of a math problem, they are in control of the information—acting on rather than reacting to it.

Number plays a greater role in literature than many self-professed "math types" or "literature types" realize. Poetry, like music, has a significant numerical component—a component exploited by mathematicians whose humorous limericks burlesque poetic form. Much contemporary science fiction, while indulging in fanciful applications, remains firmly grounded in legitimate mathematics and science.

Literature, philosophy, and mathematics intersect in works like Edwin A. Abbott's *Flatland: A Romance of Many Dimensions*.

Flatland

Part I: This World

§ I. Of the Nature of Flatland

I call our world Flatland, not because we call it so, but to make its nature clearer to you, my happy readers, who are privileged to live in Space.

Imagine a vast sheet of paper on which straight Lines, Triangles, Squares, Pentagons, Hexagons, and other figures, instead of remaining fixed on their places, move freely about, on or in the surface, but without the power of rising above or sinking below it, very much like shadows— only hard and with luminous edges—and you will then have a pretty correct notion of my country and countrymen. Alas! a few years ago, I should have said "my universe;" but now my mind has been opened to higher views of things.

In such a country, you will perceive at once that it is impossible that there should be anything of what you call a "solid" kind; but I dare say you will suppose that we could at least distinguish by sight the Triangles, Squares, and other figures moving about as I have described them. On the contrary, we could see nothing of the kind, not at least so as to distinguish one figure from another. Nothing was visible, nor could be visible, to us, except straight Lines; and the necessity of this I will speedily demonstrate.

Place a penny on the middle of one of your tables in Space; and leaning over it, look down upon it. It will appear a circle.

But now, drawing back to the edge of the table, gradually lower your eye (thus bringing yourself more and more into the condition of the inhabitants of Flatland), and you will find the penny becoming more and more oval to your view; and at last when you have placed your eye exactly on the edge of the table (so that you are, as it were, actually a Flatland citizen) the penny will then have ceased to appear oval at all, and will have become, so far as you can see, a straight line.

The same thing would happen if you were to treat in the same way a Triangle, or Square, or any other figure cut out of pasteboard. As soon as you look at it with your eye on the edge of the table, you will find that it ceases to appear to you a figure, and that it becomes in appearance a straight line. Take for example an equilateral Triangle—who represents with us a Tradesman of the respectable class. Fig. 1 represents the Tradesman as you would see him while you were bending over him from above; Figs. 2 and 3 represent the Tradesman, as you would see him if your eye were close to the level, or all but on the level of the table; and if your eye were quite on the level of the table (and that is how we see him in Flatland) you would see nothing but a straight line.

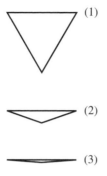

(1)

(2)

(3)

When I was in Spaceland I heard that your sailors have very similar experiences while they traverse your seas and discern some distant island or coast lying on the horizon. The far-off land may have bays, forelands, angles in and out to any number and extent; yet at a distance you see none of these (unless indeed your sun shines bright upon them revealing the projections and retirements by means of light and shade), nothing but a gray unbroken line upon the water.

Well, that is just what we see when one of our triangular or other acquaintances comes towards us in Flatland. As there is neither sun with us, nor any light of such a kind as to make shadows, we have none of the helps to the sight that you have in Spaceland. If our friend comes close to us we see his line becomes larger; if he leaves us it becomes smaller: but still he looks like a straight line; be he a Triangle, Square, Pentagon, Hexagon, Circle, what you will—a straight Line he looks and nothing else.

You may perhaps ask how under these disadvantageous circumstances we are able to distinguish our friends from one another: but the answer to this very natural question will be more fitly and easily given when I come to describe the inhabitants of Flatland. For the present let me defer this subject, and say a word or two about the climate and houses in our country. . . .

Abbott uses geometric figures to introduce philosophical questions about his own culture's *weltanschauung*—the perspective and world view of Victorian England. Teachers can use Abbott to introduce or extend geometry lessons (exploring what it means to be one dimensional, two dimensional, three dimensional, and four dimensional); to tie math study to social science topics (discussions of prejudice based on appearance or geographical origins); or to motivate math-in-art projects (drawing pictures of Flatland or Flatlanders' houses or the people of Flatland).

Other classic literature, such as folk or fairy tales, can be easily adapted to include math content and to generate math activities. "Little Red Riding Hood Turns the Times Tables on the Wolf" is my own "mathematicized" version of that popular tale.

Little Red Riding Hood Turns the Times Tables on the Wolf

Not so long ago a small girl lived in Montana near a forest. The weather was often cold—10°F at night and 30°F during the day—so the girl usually wore a red parka with a pointed hood. People called her Little Red Riding Hood after the girl in the fairy tale, or Little Red for short.

One snowy day, when school had been canceled, Little Red's mother baked four dozen chocolate chip cookies.

"The snow plows have cleared the roads," she said. "If you watch carefully for traffic, you can take these cookies and a 48-ounce jug of apple cider and visit your grandmother.

Little Red's grandmother lived in an A-frame cabin 2 miles away on the side of the mountain. Little Red enjoyed visiting her grandmother and going skiing on the mountain. Besides, she had already finished her math homework and had nothing else to do.

The girl loaded her backpack with cookies and cider, put on her red parka, and started out in the snow. It was slow going. The plows had cleared the center of the road, leaving the snow in a ridge 3 feet deep. As Little Red walked on the shoulder of the road, her boots sometimes sank a foot into the snow.

To pass the time, Little Red began repeating the multiplication tables: "2 × 2 = 4, 2 × 3 = 6, 2 × 4 = 8, 2 × 5 = 10, 2 × 6 = 12 . . ." She had gotten as far as 6 × 8 = 48 when she met a wolf.

He was sitting at the side of the road looking bored and out of sorts, like someone waiting for trouble. "Where are you going, little girl in the red parka?" he asked.

"None of your business," said Little Red, who never talked to strangers, and kept walking. But the wolf, who had nothing else to do, followed along behind.

Soon Little Red saw some friends from school shoveling snow from their driveway.

"Where are you off to?" they called.

"I'm going to my grandma's for a ski party," she called back, pointing up the mountain to her grandmother's cabin. "Want to come?"

"Sure, but we have to finish the driveway first."

"I'll help you," said Little Red; "then we can all go together, and you can help me carry all of these goodies." After a mile of walking, the 4 dozen cookies and 48-ounce jug of cider in her backpack felt like a load of bricks.

So Little Red joined her friends shoveling snow. Meanwhile, the wolf had been eavesdropping. He had seen the girl point to her grandmother's cabin. He had heard her mention goodies, and he wanted some. Racing along the road on all fours, he arrived at the cabin in less than 10 minutes. He knocked on the door—tap, tap.

"Is that you, Little Red?" called the grandmother, who was expecting her granddaughter because the mother had phoned ahead.

"Yes," croaked the wolf, sounding more like a frog than a little girl.

Thinking her granddaughter had caught a cold in the snow, the grandmother ran to the door and flung it open. The wolf leaped in, pushed the woman into the coat closet, and closed and locked the closet door.

The wolf had a plan. Not having looked at himself in a mirror recently, he thought he could dress up as the grandmother and trick the little girl into giving him all the goodies. He wrapped himself in the grandmother's size 10 housecoat, tied a chef's apron over that, and stuck the grandmother's ski cap over his ears and 2 oven mitts on his paws.

When the little girl and her friends knocked at the door, he called, "Come in," in a high voice that did not sound at all like the grandmother's.

Of course, Little Red knew immediately what had happened. She could see the wolf's head under the ski cap and his tail sticking out the back of the housecoat, and she could hear her grandmother's pounding on the door of the closet. But she decided to play along to find out what the wolf wanted.

"What big ears you have, Grandma," she said while her friends snickered behind their mittens.

"The better to hear you with, my dear," said the wolf in his fake voice.

"What big eyes you have, Grandma," said Little Red and reached outside the door for a snow shovel.

"The better to see you with, my dear," said the wolf, thinking his disguise was working.

"What big teeth you have, Grandma," said Little Red.

"The better to eat up all your goodies," said the wolf and pounced just as Little Red hit him with the snow shovel.

The girl and her friends chased the wolf outside, let Grandmother out of the coat closet, and unpacked the goodies. Then Little Red had an idea. She had noticed that her grandmother's driveway and walks needed shoveling. She guessed the wolf was the kind of animal that always ditched school and had never learned his multiplication tables.

She went to the door with a plate of cookies and called to the wolf, who was sitting on the porch and rubbing his head where the snow shovel had hit him. "Wolfie, I'll make you a deal. If you will shovel the walks and the driveway, you can have all of the cookies and cider left from our party."

The wolf was suspicious. "How do I know you will leave any," he growled.

"Figure it out for yourself," said Little Red. "We have 48 cookies and 48 ounces of cider. There are just 4 of us and we each want 2 helpings of 6 cookies and two 6-ounce mugs of cider."

The wolf, adding the numbers instead of multiplying them, thought, "4 + 2 + 6 = 12 cookies; that leaves 36 cookies for me. And 4 + 2 + 8 equals 14 ounces of cider; that leaves 34 ounces all for me."

And so while the wolf shoveled the snow, Little Red, her two friends, and her grandmother ate their two helpings of 6 cookies and drank their two mugs of hot cider.

How many cookies and how much cider were left for the wolf?

Writing to Learn Math

Throughout this book, I have recommended various writing activities for both teachers and students. As with reading, writing about mathematics helps bridge the gap between discourse in ordinary language and discourse in mathematical language. In addition, researchers have found that the writing process helps focus and refine the processing of information. Writing goals and questions at the beginning of the class focuses attention and gives purpose to inquiry. Writing summaries and comments at the end of class aids comprehension and promotes assimilation. And writing about feelings and attitudes related to math and math learning supports an integrated learning process—blending the cognitive and affective domains for a more holistic learning experience.

Writing-to-learn can supplement more traditional math lessons or help reshape math study. Supplementary writing assignments such as journals or reports extend and add depth to study by increasing the amount of time that children are actively involved with math topics and by adding another dimension to the way they look at and think about those topics. When writing-to-learn becomes an integral part of the learning process, it restructures study by effecting a more heuristic, inductive pattern of inquiry and by augmenting children's roles as inquirers, actively constructing knowledge and controlling their own learning experiences.

Math Study + Supplementary Writing

1. Teacher selects and introduces topic, motivates with activities or learning materials.
2. Teacher illustrates concepts, involves students with hands-on participation.
3. Teacher assigns problems and initiates ongoing dialogue about problem solving.
4. Student works problems, accessing learning resources to clarify concepts and to answer questions.
5. Teacher and/or student checks work; teacher and student review work, returning to resources as necessary.

6. Student writes about outcomes (affective and cognitive) in learning journal, researches math concepts or math personalities for a written report, explores ways of assimilating new information and integrating with previous knowledge and skills.

Writing-Based Math Study

1. Student selects concept or area for study and composes questions or topics to focus work.
2. Student seeks answers to questions or information about topics from books, computer programs, instructors, and so forth.
3. Student summarizes information, defines terms, outlines processes.
4. Student experiments, applying concepts in problem solving.
5. Student checks and reviews work, composing explanations for outcomes (correct or incorrect) and, if necessary, accessing learning resources for additional material.
6. Student writes about outcomes (affective and cognitive) in learning journal; researches math concepts or math personalities for a written report; explores ways of assimilating new information and integrating with previous knowledge and skills.

In the first pattern, writing might be used to motivate at the beginning of study and also to clarify concepts as a part of problem solving. But for the most part writing comes at the end of study as students rethink *what* they have learned and *how* they have learned it. In the second pattern, writing in effect provides an envelope for math study, not only beginning and ending the process but also generating and shaping the process itself.

Whether teachers should use writing to supplement or to structure the study of math depends on the curriculum, children's preferred learning styles, and teaching styles. In either case, the writing usually will fall into three basic categories: expository, expressive, and creative writing.

1. *Expository writing:* Basically, expository writing is writing that explains. Summaries, paraphrases, reports, outlines, definitions, questions—all reinforce learning and keep information active. Moreover, writing is essentially a proprietary act. When students put information in their own words, they exercise control over both the information itself and their learning; thus writing (like the strategies discussed in the next chapter) works to empower students to learn mathematics.

2. *Expressive writing:* The focus of expressive writing is attitudes—positive and negative emotions and their effect on the learning process. Expressive writing about math includes learning-journal entries that explore anxieties, dialogues that reprise emotionally charged learning experiences, cathartic effusions with titles like "Why I Hate (or Love) Fractions," and freewriting about feelings.

Some process writing can be both expository and expressive. For example, metacognitive writing that records the thought processes will include explorations of concepts and attitudes. Also dialectical writing, such as double-entry notebooks, asks students first to write exposition, reporting on the content of a book or learning activity, and then to write expressively, responding to content, context, and implications.

3. *Creative writing:* Creative writing is less personal than expressive writing but more informal than expository writing. Stories, poems, or plays can be written about math concepts or math attitudes or both. Some of the math play in Chapter 8, such as cloze puzzles, and the math reading discussed earlier, such as original or adapted stories, actually started with teachers' creative writing about math, but children can also create their own games and readings. An effective story-writing activity begins with the question: "What if?"

"What if you had $5.00 and you went to the mall to buy a _____ that cost _____?"
"What if you wanted to go on a class trip to _____, and you needed $_____?"
"What if you shrank to 1/10 of your current size?"

Creative activities work equally well as collaborative or individual assignments. In either case, they help children to verbalize and contextualize concepts—essential skills for problem solving—and, most important, to "think" math—that is, to take math ideas and language out of the math lesson hour and make them part of real-time thinking, speaking, and acting.

Significantly, writing-to-learn-math shifts the pedagogical focus from product to process. When students record how they solved a problem as well as the solution itself, the teacher's response automatically broadens from whether the solution is correct or incorrect to why the problem-solving process worked or did not work. Good math teaching has always emphasized the how's and why's of problem solving. But "explain what you did" leads to a clearer picture of thought processes than "show all your work."

Among math specialists, the most common objections to reading and writing to learn math begin with, "We're not trained to teach reading and writing." The statement underscores two major problems in our educational system: overspecialization and territoriality. For the most part, in elementary school the pursuit of knowledge has not yet been fragmented and compartmentalized, with one room and teacher for math, another for English, another for science, and so forth; therefore, across-curriculum approaches not only fit but also can function with a minimum of upheaval. Children who experience math study as part of rather than separate from the total educational experience are less likely to see math as extraordinary or intimidating. Reading and writing to learn math in elementary school can establish children's patterns for processing math information before our educational system imposes its artificial barriers.

Questions for Thought and Discussion

1. Have you ever studied math using the reading-and-writing-to-learn methods discussed in this chapter? If so, what were the results? If not, have you taken any courses that might have been improved by these methods?
2. Have you ever used reading-and-writing-to-learn in teaching mathematics? If so, what were the results? If not, would you like to do so in the future?
3. Which methods might work best for you as a learner? As a teacher? Would any of the methods not fit your learning and teaching styles or your school's curriculum?
4. How might reading-and-writing-to-learn impact children's attitudes about mathematics and their performance on the objectives of a standard mathematics curriculum?

Activities

1. Adapt a favorite folk or fairy tale to emphasize numbers or math concepts. For example, you might add measurements to a tall tale about Paul Bunyan and his giant blue ox or the story of Pecos Bill, whose spurs supposedly created the Rio Grande rift. When you have completed the adaptation, ask a group of students or colleagues to read it and answer these questions: What is the story about? What do the numbers or math content add to the meaning of the story?
2. Write two versions of a math lesson—one in math language and one in ordinary language—following the examples given in this chapter. Give each version to a different group of students who have not previously studied the concept; then ask them to apply what they have learned to a set of 25 to 50 exercise problems. Which group's performance is better? Do the groups' reactions to the lessons differ? Do the students seem anxious or confident? Actively involved in learning or passive and disinterested?

Annotated List of Readings

Abbott, Edwin A. *Flatland: A Romance of Many Dimensions.* Boston: Little, Brown, 1937 ed. *Satiric fantasy, exploring the world of space-time. Uses geometric images to pose philosophical questions about the universe, its inhabitants, and our perceptions of reality (or realities).*

Connolly, Paul, and Teresa Vilardi, eds. *Writing to Learn Mathematics and Science.* New York: Teachers College Press, 1989. *Collection of essays about using writing to teach mathematics and science. Presents rationale and methods and argues for the use of writing at all levels of mathematics instruction.*

10

Empowering Students to Learn Math

Empowerment has become an important political word, but it is equally significant for education. Empowering students to learn means freeing them from conditions that have limited or restricted learning and at the same time giving them owners' rights to the subject. *Every student has a right to learn math.* The obligations that go with that right include the students' obligation to master the subject and the teacher's obligation to make mastery possible.

Some proponents of empowerment take it a step further and turn learning a subject lock, stock, and barrel over to the students. Students decide what, when, where, and how they will learn. One graduate of this type of education calls it the "jungle gym" system of learning because it allows children to skip the basics and major, as he did, in playground and jungle gym activities.

Empowering students without obviating a teacher's responsibilities requires a balance between student and teacher control: not a classroom democracy but shared power and responsibility where sharing furthers the students' best interests. Empowerment that works in the classroom must empower students without disenfranchising teachers, reinforce rather than undermine the curriculum, and lighten rather than increase teachers' loads. In the math classroom specifically, empowerment must occur within the contexts described by this book—acknowledging and treating teachers' and even parents' math anxieties, preventing math anxiety and promoting math confidence in students, and responding to the sometimes intimidating importance of numbers in our lives and society.

How can teachers motivate without intimidation? How can we accelerate and individualize learning without overloading teachers? How can we apply a constructivist (in a Piagetian sense, as used in Chapter 6, rather than a more radical version), bottom-up approach to learning without losing control of the class's progress or losing sight of curriculum objectives? Those are the key questions. Two possible answers involve learning systems and learning technologies.

Empowering Students through Learning Systems

Some years ago I did my student teaching under the supervision of a veteran math teacher. Young and idealistic, I tended, according to my mentor, to "spoon-feed" students. I micromanaged every detail of the class, spent hours tutoring and more hours grading daily homework assignments and the multiple test forms that I used to give students second and third chances not only to pass but also to improve their performances. The result? My students liked math and earned high grades. They also became extremely dependent on me and my methods. Reportedly, their next math class was a shock both to them and to the teacher.

The problem was not so much spoon-feeding—breaking the subject into manageable bites and taking them one at a time—as force-feeding. Constant effort, continual feedback, the try-try-try-again approach to testing—all worked to promote learning in a positive, supportive environment. However, my micromanaging placed me firmly in the driver's seat; the students came along for the ride.

From this experience and others emerged a system that I call Student Managed Mastery Learning or SMML. The system combines some objectives and methods of traditional mastery learning with collaborative-learning strategies. Teachers maintain control of learning objectives and outcomes, but they share with students control of the learning process, including evaluation. In practical terms, this means increasing student activity and effort without increasing teaching duties. It also means that students who respond well to spoon-fed mathematics can be accommodated by spoon-feeding themselves or each other and still not develop an overly teacher-dependent learning style.

Adapting the Objectives and Methods of Mastery Learning

Mastery learning and personalized systems of instruction are, of course, neither new nor, in themselves, effective deterrents to math anxiety. A local community college relies wholly on a mastery-learning system in its basic math program. Students study in classes or computerized learning labs, as they choose, but their grades depend on performance on the mastery tests, administered by the testing center. This system will work for approximately 30 percent of the students—those who study intensely for the first test form and use the other two forms as a safety net. The other 70 percent will use the first test form as a trial run and approach the other two forms as last-ditch attempts. The result, predictably, is that the intensely studious 30 percent experience an accompanying increase in confidence over the course of the semester, while their less fortunate companions, the remaining 70 percent, become

FIGURE 10-1   Comparison of ML and SMML Learning Systems

Components	Traditional ML	SMML
Objectives	Defined in terms of behavior	Defined in cognitive and affective terms
Motivation	External	Internal
Instructional materials	Emphasis on programmed instruction, deduction, ready-made knowledge to be transmitted	Mixture of show and tell, induction and deduction, knowledge to be discovered and constructed, knowledge to be transmitted
Instructional focus	Personalized	Personalized plus collaborative
Pacing	Personalized	Personalized plus collaborative
Teacher's role	Systems management—provide materials, monitor progress, diagnose problems, remediate, motivate, provide feedback on homework and tests, evaluate outcomes	Teaching system overview—set goals, evaluate progress and outcomes, praise and encourage
Student's role	Learning	Learning and sharing systems management—select materials, diagnose problems and seek remediation, monitor progress, self-motivate, correct homework and tests, self-evaluate
Outcomes	Mastery-level scores (80% or higher) on battery of tests	Mastery-level scores (percentage chosen by teacher) on battery of tests; confidence about math learning; demonstration of variety of problem-solving processes and facility in matching process to problem; development of cognitive structures essential to math learning

more and more anxious over the same period. I counseled one adult student who, after three tries at the class, had regressed from anxiety to dysfunction, from passing some forms to passing none.

The differences between traditional mastery learning (ML) and my Student Managed Mastery Learning System are summarized in Figure 10-1 above. Basically, SMML holds to several underlying principles of traditional mastery and personalized systems of instruction:

1. Setting specific goals and objectives for learning
2. Allowing for differences in pace of learning
3. Providing compensatory instruction where needed
4. Providing multiple opportunities to succeed
5. Individualizing learning plans

Potentially, these principles should lead to humane and humanized math instruction. In practice, many traditional mastery-learning programs (like the one in our community college) have overemphasized the system, fitting students to the system rather than the system to the students, while at the same time reducing the teacher's role from professional educator to technician and system manager. In 1968 Fred Keller published "Good-bye Teacher . . .," his influential article articulating the benefits of mastery-learning systems. Depicting education as a factory, Keller insisted that the factory's production depended on its materials and systems, that teachers' efforts rated no higher than 10% efficiency, and that teachers' energies should be devoted to procedures and paperwork. Twenty years later, my counterargument appeared in the *American Journal of Education:* "Hello Teacher: An Argument for Reemphasizing the Teacher's Role in PSI and Mastery Learning." Basically, I argued that teachers and good teaching have always been essential parts of classroom learning—even in PSI and mastery-learning programs where researchers' biases have ignored teachers' contributions. Reemphasizing the teacher's role means not only giving teachers credit but also freeing them to teach—to take an active, creative role in the learning process.

SMML does this in part by rearranging responsibilities. Any mastery or personalized system of instruction is going to be labor-intensive. Providing feedback, scoring multiple test forms, compensating, remediating, monitoring, motivating— micromanaging dozens of details in dozens of variations to fit dozens of students consumes time and energy, even in computerized or computer-supported classrooms. In SMML, students micromanage; teachers macromanage (see Figure 10-1).

SMML empowers students by placing them in charge of information. When students score their own homework or tests, they become insiders—sharers in the mysteries and rites of evaluation. SMML also empowers students by giving them some control over the learning process. Monitoring their own progress, deciding what to study and what to review, when to seek and when to give help move students from the realm of acted on to acting and begin the development of metacognitive skills; students not only think about math but also think about thinking about math.

Within this context of shared control, repeatable testing becomes a strong deterrent to math anxiety. Why might children (or adults) feel anxious about math tests? Because they fear and in some cases even anticipate failure. For some, the potential for public failure—a low score marked clearly in red at the top of a test paper—compounds the distress. The opportunity to retest makes the consequences of any single test less threatening. In addition, when I use repeatable testing, I like to go a step further and offer, not just chances to avoid failure, but opportunities to succeed. I do this by rewarding the retester. While some programs call for averaging all tests or limiting the score on a repeated test to a low pass, mine calls for acknowledging the highest level of accomplishment. If a student scores an "F" on the first test form, a "C" on the second, and an "A" on the third, the grade is an "A." A student who scores a "B" on the first form and wants to earn an "A" can still repeat the form. The system, of course, encourages retesting and sometimes results in more high grades than proponents of the bell curve might approve. However, the students themselves help with the extra grading, and the grades are earned on standards of mastery instead of relative standing in a class.

Mixing Personalized and Collaborative Learning

A serious weakness of most mastery and personalized systems has been the isolation of the learner. Working alone according to an individualized study plan lets students progress at their own rate and lets teachers tailor instructional packages to special needs, but it also restricts the individual's opportunities to learn. In education, the total truly is greater than the sum of its parts, and several heads are generally better than one. We can make the same criticism of computer-based education. At a small college in the 1980s, I taught a student who had transferred from an experimental school. All the basic skills in that school, especially math and English, were taught by computers in open-entry, open-exit courses. Despite state-of-the-art equipment and excellent software, the experiment failed. As my student put it, "It was too lonesome, and we weren't learning anything." In other words, as social beings, the students needed the social interaction and collaboration of classroom learning.

Learning together complements individualized learning in several ways.

1. By laying the groundwork for individual study
2. By establishing a support group for encouragement
3. By establishing a resource group for questions and clarifications
4. By multiplying the number of students working on a topic, thereby increasing the potential for understanding

The action pattern for an SMML activity might look something like a revolving pinwheel. The teacher initiates study with a group lesson or activity; then students diverge, working with the material, interacting with each other and the teacher when they have questions or problems, but centering on a concept or group of concepts.

Empowering Students through Technology

Many teachers think of classroom technology as a post-1970s phenomenon of the personal-computer age. In fact, the word *Technology* (with a capital *T*) connotes high-tech equipment; push-button learning, and artificial intelligences—the stuff of sci-fi movies and futuristic daydreams. Math education specialists in particular have hailed the new technologies as the solution to math teaching's perennial problem: how to teach mathematics thoroughly and effectively to students who may or may not want to learn math. According to math-methods types, because math teachers have generally been ineffective in the math classroom in the past, they should not try to teach math at all; instead, they should let machines do the teaching.

This don't-teach philosophy relies on two basic axioms—that the best math teacher is a computer and that computer instruction somehow guarantees maximum learning for the maximum number of students. A colleague who has adopted this view claims, "Technology has already made classroom teachers obsolete. By the year 2025 it will have made schools obsolete." He envisions students studying at home on PCs, progress coordinated from a computer center, and teaching staff reduced to a few experts needed to write the software and a few technicians needed to keep the system running.

The idea is roughly analogous to the idea that schools could have been eliminated in the sixteenth century because the printing press had made books and knowledge accessible to everyone, or in the 1950s because televison and televised instruction could reach every home. Instead of replacing schools and teachers, technology and its products, such as books, have in the past and will in the future expand the potentials for teaching and learning. It is not so much *what* technology we use as *how* we use it that has the greatest impact on education.

Empowering students with technology means, on the one hand, teaching them to use its tools and products effectively and, on the other, teaching them to control the technology they use rather than being controlled by it. Students are controlling technology when:

1. They use it to increase their productivity—to study more concepts and study them in, perhaps, different ways; to do more exercises; to take more tests.
2. They use it to find answers to questions and to develop more questions to find answers for.
3. They use it metacognitively—that is, to evaluate their own work, rate their own progress, diagnose their own problems and seek assistance.
4. They use it to do repetitive tasks more quickly and effectively.
5. They use it to extend and expand the learning period—for example, to do homework.

Students are being controlled by technology when:

1. Learning mechanical procedures (to push buttons or give commands) or previously learned algorithms take the place of learning concepts or developing thinking skills.
2. Technology defines the parameters of the learning experience, dictating learning style and conditions (if you find yourself saying that you cannot solve this

or that problem because the available software doesn't consider this or that variation—and it doesn't occur to you to try something else—you're allowing the technology sitting in front of you to limit your options).

3. Technology restricts flexibility in performance.
4. Students cannot do the work—solve a problem, illustrate a concept, check an answer—without technology.

Empowerment means establishing and exercising ownership and control. Being controlled is more than an opposite condition; it is an opposing spiral of decreasing power and increasing limitations. Theorists who advocate eliminating basic and even advanced mathematics from the school curriculum sometimes couch their arguments in the language of empowerment. Freeing students from learning arithmetic, they say, allows more time for creative mathematics and problem solving. But *not* learning arithmetic—or algebra or trigonometry or calculus—frees no one. Owning a calculator or computer that can perform mathematical functions is not the same thing as being able to perform the operations—that is, owning and using the information itself.

Several years ago I attempted to teach college math to a young man who had learned what I call calculator arithmetic. He could manipulate the calculator to solve problems, but he could not explain what the calculator was doing or do the operations himself. He could not estimate answers or recognize errors; he could do some addition and subtraction but little multiplication and division and no square roots or problems involving decimals. He had little math knowledge and few math skills, and he was extremely math anxious—distressed and restricted by the so-called freedom from learning that an innovative program in a private school had substituted for a basic math curriculum.

When to Use Calculators and When Not to Use Them

While computers are more high-profile and trendy, calculators continue to be the most versatile technological tool for elementary math classes. "Have calculator, will calculate" could be the slogan for many basic math classes. Because the calculator is inexpensive, most students can have their own—part of their school supplies, like crayons and spiral notebooks. Because the calculator is mobile, its effectiveness extends outside the classroom and away from the computer station for field projects and group activities.

Calculators help empower children to learn math when they are used as tools rather than substitutes for learning. Remember the central ritual of traditional pencil-and-paper math instruction? Students worked exercises or test problems, handed them in, then waited anxiously for the teacher to mark the papers and record the scores. The longer the time elapsed, the greater the anxiety about the score and the less students remembered about the problems themselves. Enabling children to check their own answers, to have access to solutions without waiting on a teacher-oracle's convenience, empowers them in two ways: first, it transfers ownership of the "right" answers from teacher to students; second, it increases the potential for learning by removing the feedback glitch in students' information-processing system. That is, if they can confirm accuracy during different steps in the problem-solving process, they can keep the information alive in working memory for a longer period of time and ensure the storage of more information and more accurate information in long-term memory at the end of a working session.

Teachers, of course, are not the only ones tempted to substitute button pushing for problem solving. Ensuring that calculators are used as tools rather than learning substitutes requires a shift in focus from show-the-right-answer exercises to show-a-solution activities. Too often, teachers as well as students have lost sight of process in their concern for answer-book products. I can remember in my own grade school days arguing with my teachers about answers. The nuns who taught math at the parochial schools that I attended taught all of us to respect authority. If the answer book said one thing and our calculations showed something different, the answer in the book was considered correct. I learned early to "prove" my answers in as many different ways as possible. Those experiences taught me that a disembodied product means nothing; it takes process and product together to make a convincing solution. Now I sometimes give students pages from textbook answer books and ask them to check for accuracy. Not surprisingly, my students at all levels, from basic math to advanced statistics, have found errors. At the same time, they develop an appreciation for the importance of process and a respect for their own problem-solving abilities.

The exercises that follow illustrate some ways that calculators can be used effectively in math learning. On the one hand, the activities let students take advantage of the calculator's ability to provide correct answers; on the other hand, they demonstrate that problem solving is cognitive, not mechanical. It relies on good thinking, not quick fingers.

Math with Calculators: Activity #1

Objective: Students discover the capabilities and the limitations of their calculators.

Procedure: Working either with printed sheets or a chalkboard, the teacher leads the students through a series of exercises. The first set demonstrate what their calculators can do:

1. $\begin{array}{r} 45 \\ + 26 \\ \hline \end{array}$ 2. $\begin{array}{r} 45 \\ \times 48 \\ \hline \end{array}$ 3. $45 \times 45 \times 45 =$ 4. $91125 \div 45 =$

5. $\begin{array}{r} 18999 \\ - 6333 \\ \hline \end{array}$ 6. $\sqrt{3136}$ 7. 3% of 58 $=$

The second set demonstrate what they cannot do:

1. Show *how* 45, 54, 109, and 5 are added for a total of 213.
2. Show *how* 4095 divided by 63 equals 65.
3. Find the cause of the errors in:

   $$45 + 26 + 15 = 76 \qquad 55 + 26 + 104 = 175$$
   $$39 + 39 + 39 = 971 \qquad 63 \times 5 = 305$$
   $$29 \times 15 = 395$$
4. Solve without rounding for more digits than on the display.
5. Do simple computations more quickly with calculators than they can be done mentally.

Outcomes: Students learn to use calculators critically, to make using calculators part of the problem-solving process rather than the whole process. (The activity can work with all levels using calculators if the teacher varies the difficulty of the exercises to fit the groups.)

Math with Calculators: Activity #2

Objective: Students compare mental, hand (pencil-and-paper), and calculator problem solving for speed and ability to deal with complex situations.

Procedure: The teacher divides the class into teams—a team to use calculators, a team to use pencil and paper, and a team to do calculations in their heads. There should be a record keeper with a stopwatch for each team. Both the accuracy of answers and the time to compute should be recorded for each problem.

The teacher can start with single-digit problems, then move to double and triple digits. To test ability to deal with complex operations, the teacher can hand out written exercise sheets with number puzzles or word problems. (The teacher will want to make a distinction between complicated but linear computations—such as $1112 - 12 \times 6 - 48 + 523 \times 4$—and complex problems such as $4(120 - 70) \div 8$ ($150 - 50) \times 6$.)

Outcomes: Students learn when to use calculators to advantage and also develop confidence in their own calculating abilities.

When to Use Computers and When Not to Use Them

People, not computers, are the best math teachers. Creativity, spontaneity, integrating affective and cognitive domains, assessing cause as well as effect and process as well as product, displaying human interest and humane caring—these essential ingredients of the art (rather than the science) of teaching are either beyond the scope of the machine or, at best, are present in a static, two-dimensional sense, reflecting the humanity and skill of programmers. Nonetheless, computers make excellent teachers' aides. They interact, they tirelessly repeat the same information, and, within certain limitations, they can answer an endless stream of questions.

What I am saying, of course, is that I believe in CAI, computer-assisted instruction, but not CBI, computer-based instruction. Teaching math with computers empowers both the students and the teacher when the computer takes over repetitive chores and provides one-to-one instructional support. But a word of caution: Computerized math teaching can restrict student learning and alter the teacher's role from professional to technician.

Figure 10-2 below compares computer-assisted and computer-based instructional systems. Basically, CAI uses the computer as a tool—one medium among many for learning—whereas CBI limits learning to one system. CAI can work with a few classroom computers or trips to a computer lab; CBI requires a PC for each student. CAI allows for one-to-one tutoring in overcrowded classrooms, frees the teacher to teach creatively and humanely, and lets students control the pace of learn-

FIGURE 10-2   Comparison of Computer Learning Systems

CAI (Computer-Assisted Instruction)	*CBI (Computer-Based Instruction)*
1. Computer backs up other systems of instructional delivery.	1. Computer is primary system for instructional delivery.
2. Classroom instruction focuses on group learning; computer tutoring is individualized.	2. Learning is completely individualized.
3. Computer assists with backup testing and scoring—such as repeatable testing forms in mastery learning.	3. Computer tests, scores, and keeps records for each student's learning program.
4. Teacher initiates study, motivates, guides activities, monitors progress, answers questions about subject or about computer use.	4. Computer initiates study, motivates, guides activities, monitors progress; teacher maintains discipline, oversees work, answers questions about computer use.
5. Machine–student interaction alternates with teacher–student and student–student interaction.	5. Student interacts primarily with machine.
6. Standardized computer instruction is mixed with nonstandardized classroom instruction.	6. Instruction, materials, and evaluation are standardized.
7. Students work in many media.	7. Students work in one medium.
8. Teachers set goals and evaluate outcomes.	8. Computer program sets goals and evaluates outcomes.

ing and the number of repetitions; CBI isolates the student, making learning linear and two-dimensional. Interestingly, at a time when cognitive development has become the focus of most educators, some technologists are urging math teachers in particular to rely almost exclusively on CBI. No matter how sophisticated, computer instruction is programmed instruction, and programmed instruction is one application of behavioristic learning theory. Behaviorism still has a place in the classroom, but letting it control learning limits the development of higher cognitive skills and restricts critical thinking.

Some guidelines follow for using without abusing computerized math instruction:

USE computers to reinforce class activities and lessons.
USE computers to perform repetitive tasks.
USE computers to vary the instructional medium.
USE computers for math games and fun.
USE computers for catch-up and make-up work.

DO NOT USE computers to replace class activities and lessons.
DO NOT USE computers to replace teacher–student interaction.
DO NOT USE computers to replace student–student interaction.
DO NOT USE computers to replace teacher evaluation.
DO NOT USE computers to replace all books and hands-on learning materials.

Questions for Thought and Discussion

1. What does it mean to empower someone to learn?
2. How might empowering students influence the affective domain of learning? The eustress/distress poles of stress? Math anxiety and math confidence?
3. How do you feel about technology in the classroom? Are we overusing or underusing technology?
4. What is behaviorism? What is its place in classroom learning?
5. What does it mean to *master* a subject? How might a mastery system affect the affective and cognitive domains of learning?

Activities

1. Conduct a teacher research project to assess the advantages of SMML or another mastery-learning system. For several weeks, record the results of the current system in student progress, attitude, and so forth. Then implement a mastery system and record the results for the same number of weeks. Analyze and compare the data. Why do you think the results are or are not significantly different?
2. Do a survey of technology in your school. What equipment does the school have? How is it used—ways, means, frequencies, and so forth? Are these uses empowering to students and to teachers? Make a plan for using the available technology effectively in math instruction.

Annotated List of Readings

Keller, Fred. "Goodbye Teacher . . ." *Journal of Applied Behavior Analysis 1* (1968): 79–89. *Classic article in the field of mastery learning and PSI. Restricts teacher's role to classroom technician.*

Martinez, Joseph G. R., and Nancy C. Martinez. "Hello Teacher: An Argument for Reemphasizing the Teacher's Role in PSI and Mastery Learning." *American Journal of Education 97,* no. 1 (1988): 18–33. *Response to Keller's article. Reasserts the importance of good teaching and good teachers.*

Schepp, Debra, and Brad Schepp. *Computer Club!* New York: Windcrest/McGraw-Hill, 1994. *Introduction of Shareware, six software programs that use computer games to instruct. Includes several math games.*

Papert, Seymour. *The Children's Machine: Rethinking School in the Age of the Computer.* New York: HarperCollins Basic Books, 1993. *Constructivist approach to computers' role in education. Contrasts with my views and places computers at center stage in instruction.*

11

Mathematics Is an Equal-Opportunity Subject

Mathematics in the Media #1

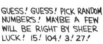

Mathematics in the Media #2

FOX TROT © 1994 Bill Amend.

Mathematics in the Media #3

Stand and Deliver

A group of students from an East Los Angeles high school take the Educational Testing Service advanced-placement examination for calculus. All of the students pass the exam, several with extremely high scores. Because the students are all Hispanic, because the school generally scores lower on the standardized tests than schools in more affluent parts of the city, ETS accuses the students of cheating, disallows their scores, and forces them to retest.

Of the three media examples, only the first one is politically correct, but all are true nonetheless. In the first grade, boys are as likely as girls to have problems learning math. By high school, girls are more likely to avoid math courses, and minority group members of both genders are expected to take remedial rather than advanced math courses.

Why? Are girls less able to learn math? Are minorities as products of Third World cultures somehow unsuited by nature to study Western civilization's most elite subject? Is mathematics a First World subject at all? Did the ideas and concepts associated with the traditional math curriculum emerge from the Western march of progress that purportedly began in Greece and Rome; skipped the Dark Ages; then moved steadily through Europe during the Renaissance, the Enlightenment, and the Industrial Revolution? Is math, in short, a subject of, by, and for white, majority-culture males?

The answer to all of these questions is a resounding *no* followed by an equally resounding *but.* No, nature does not give white males an advantage in learning math, and, no, mathematics is not an exclusively Western subject; it is the product of learning and cultures worldwide. But nurture—what is experienced as opposed to what is inherited—writes a different story. Everyone *can* learn math; math learning ability observes no racial, ethnic, or gender boundaries. But some people learn (or are taught) *not* to learn math.

Several years ago I participated in a curriculum development project at a Bureau of Indian Affairs (BIA) boarding school. My own background mixes Hispanic with Native American cultures; therefore, I approached the project with some strong opinions about what should be taught and how it should be taught. Specifically, I argued for a strong, challenging curriculum—one that would give the students an advantage rather than place them at a disadvantage. Some of the teaching staff agreed with me, but most did not; and the majority ruled. Because they were caring, sensitive teachers, concerned about the children as people as well as students, they wanted a curriculum that would not "damage fragile self-esteem," "overtax and discourage," "overemphasize a subject foreign to Native American cultures and backgrounds."

It was a case of being wrong for all the right reasons. These were dedicated teachers. They wanted what was best for their Native American students, *but they did not really believe in those students.* In fact, their caring and concern hid a stereotype of Native Americans as artistic rather than quantitative types; it also hid some ugly basic assumptions—that Native Americans *cannot* learn math as well as Anglo children; that lack of pride and self-respect cripples their ability to face learning challenges; and that their racial identity somehow disqualifies them to compete or participate in a modern, numbers-driven society. Of course, these assumptions fuel self-fulfilling prophecies and have an impact on decisions. These teachers demanded a watered-down math curriculum because they did not believe the children could meet the challenge of an accelerated or even a standard math program. Such a watered-down curriculum guarantees failure, frustration, and math anxiety when students who are products of such curricula encounter the real thing in college, technical schools, or the working world.

Discovering Stereotypes in Math Teaching and Learning

We all stereotype others to some extent. When we call a friend a "control freak" or a supervisor a "Type A personality," we are stereotyping. When we justify a spending binge or a tendency to procrastinate as the effect of an astrological sign or a type of upbringing, we are stereotyping. When I avoid a trip to the opera because I am a "math type" rather than an "artistic type," or an afternoon tea because I am not the "tea-and-crumpets type," I am stereotyping. Some stereotyping is harmless, some even fun. However, when the stereotypes affect curriculum and pedagogy, they require assessment, diagnosis, and remediation.

In math teaching specifically, some stereotypes come disguised as contemporary wisdom. The obvious one is the idea that boys are inherently math types, whereas girls must be lured from a natural affinity with the arts to study math and science. Less obvious are stereotypes that come roughly under the headings of "knowing your limits" and "emphasizing your students' strengths":

> "I'm a creative, not a quantitative type; therefore, I'll let the computer teach math."
>
> "Merrill is artistic like most Native Americans; therefore, it doesn't matter if he can't do math."
>
> "For a math activity, the girls can research and write about the history of math while the boys design and build a mini-computer."
>
> "Orientals are good at math, while Blacks and Hispanics are not, so I'll create a remedial math group and put Lee Wong in charge."
>
> "Teresa and Suzanne performed poorly on their math quizzes, but their essays were good. I'll praise them for their writing and downplay their math."

Notice that none of these statements connotes ill will or intentional putdowns. Nevertheless, all present subtle cues that define limits for math learning. The activities and test in Figures 11-1 (page 144) and 11-2 (page 145) will help you assess your own math stereotyping. As you analyze your own behaviors and attitudes, remember that stereotyping is harmful if it prejudges abilities, likes, or needs; limits or restricts learning or perceptions of learning outcomes; and teaches students to limit or restrict their own learning.

Teachers are not the only ones who stereotype; students may also generalize and label themselves and each other. "Math dumb," "math nerd," "numbers junky," "computer jerk," "computer geek," "brainiac," "arithmenut"—few teachers use names like these, but students do. And when they name-call, they are stereotyping. I am often amazed at how early children begin stereotyping each other and accepting stereotypes of themselves. Fourth- and fifth-grade girls neglect math because it is a "boys' subject." Fourth- and fifth-grade boys fall into the good-at-math/poor-at-English-and-reading type of either-or thinking.

Identifying harmful stereotypes in children's self-images and perceptions of others calls for some teacher research. Self-tests, as we have seen before, have limited usefulness with elementary-level children because of their limited metacognitive skills. They may, in fact, act one way and say something else, or behave one way but interpret their behavior in a different way. Since effects rather than causes are children's strong points, we can begin at the end, then probe backward for reasons. The student survey in Figure 11-3 on page 145 consists of beginning-point questions. The teacher asks the question, then uses the answer to generate other questions in an open-ended string. Once an entire class has been surveyed orally, the teacher can review the results, looking for patterns and red flags. For example, expressions such as "everyone knows," "everyone does it," "all girls," "a guy-thing," "sissy stuff" point toward the intrusion of hasty generalizations, a fallacy that promotes stereotyping in children's thinking processes. Name calling and explaining performance in gender or ethnic terms are also red flags. Potentially harmful

FIGURE 11-1   Teachers' Stereotyping Self-Test

Check the *Yes* or the *No* column for each question. Eight or more checks in the *Yes* column indicates a serious stereotyping problem; four to seven, a problem; and any, the need for corrective action.

	Yes	*No*
1. Have you ever excused poor math performance or attitude by saying that you (or your students) are right-brained and creative rather than left-brained and quantitative?	___	___
2. Do you expect more from boys than girls in math class?	___	___
3. Close your eyes and call to mind the image of the quintessential math whiz. Is the image a boy?	___	___
4. Close your eyes and call to mind the image of a great mathematician. Is the image male?	___	___
5. Have you ever praised ethnic students for assumed group traits—blacks for good athletic ability, Native Americans for artistic ability, Hispanics for musical abilities, and so forth?	___	___
6. Do you call on boys more often than girls to do math problems?	___	___
7. Do you call on girls more often than boys during writing or reading lessons?	___	___
8. Have you ever attributed poor or good math performance to ethnicity—that is, to Asians' supposed facility with numbers, to Native Americans' supposed problems in dealing with time, and so forth?	___	___
9. Fill in the blanks in the following sentence with the first words that come to mind: _____ is a Ph.D. in mathematics; _____ supervises a computer lab. Does the first word refer to a male? Does the second word refer to a male?	___	___
10. Fill in the blanks in the following sentence with the first words that come to mind: _____ hates math; _____ is very math maxious. Does the first word refer to a female? Does the second word refer to a female?	___ ___	___ ___

FIGURE 11-2   Teachers' Self-Discovery Activities

1. Have a friend or colleague observe your class when you teach a math lesson. Have the observer tally and time your interchanges by gender—number of times you call on boys and girls, time you give them to answer questions, length of your own responses to their questions or comments. Continue the observations for several days. Then assess the results. Look for patterns and trends. Do you call on girls or boys more often? Do you give them equal time to answer questions?
2. At the beginning of the school year, before you know the students well, write down your predictions for their performance in math. Several months into the year, review your predictions and speculate about the basis for your first impressions and assumptions about math-learning ability.
3. Explore your assumptions about math-learning ability in a freewriting activity. Time the activity (15 minutes, 30 minutes, etc.), and write continuously. (Don't worry about sentence structure, spelling, or grammar.) At the end of the period, review what you have written. Are there any surprises?

FIGURE 11-3   Survey of Stereotyping and Potential for Stereotyping in Children's Thought Processes and Behaviors

This is an oral survey to be administered individually in nonthreatening settings. Use the answers to each question to generate more questions. If possible, tape each session and prepare a transcript rather than trying to write down responses during the interview itself.

1. Do you like math?
2. Do most girls like math?
3. Do boys like math?
4. Which members of your family like math?
5. Who is the best mathematician in your class?
6. Do you think (insert name of minority classmate) is good at math?
7. Repeat question #6 until all ethnic or racial groups in the class have been represented.
8. Who do you think is smarter, a mathematician from the United States or a mathematician from Egypt? From Mexico? From India? From China?
9. Who is the worst mathematician in your class?
10. Who has the hardest job—a math teacher, a reading teacher, or an English teacher?

patterns might include several children's saying that boys like math but girls do not, that a specific minority group or minorities in general are not good at math, or that U.S. mathematicians are smarter than mathematicians in other countries.

Eliminating Stereotypes in Math Teaching and Learning

Identifying stereotypes is the easy part; freeing your own math teaching and your students' math learning of stereotypes is harder—but not impossible. First, of course, there must be a will to change. Teachers must be convinced that the problem is serious enough to warrant commitment and effort. Consider the following case studies.

Case Study #1

The subject is a Hispanic male who attended parochial schools. In elementary school, he had trouble with basic arithmetic. The teacher dealt with his problem by giving him more attention, but in a public way—calling on him or sending him to the chalkboard more often. The result was a downward spiral of poor performances, bad attitudes, and math anxiety. Eventually his classmates labeled him "math dumb," and the teacher told him he would not be "college material" because of his poor math skills.

 Throughout high school the subject avoided math, taking only the required survival courses instead of college-prep courses. However, because of open-admissions policies in the 1960s, he was admitted to college. There he discovered an affinity for the life sciences. Excelling in all but the quantitative parts of his studies—A's in biology, C's and below in math, physics, and chemistry—he earned a degree with teacher certification in life science. But, when a professor who had been impressed by his abilities arranged for a graduate research fellowship, he turned it down. A master's degree, he explained, required more math, and—"If I couldn't learn math in twelve years of grade school and high school, I certainly can't learn it in a semester or two of college."

Case Study #2

The subject is a female. She had no problems with elementary school math but began to struggle in middle school. On the basis of achievement test scores, a school counselor advised her to focus on her strengths—the humanities, especially languages. Nevertheless, the subject continued to take math and science courses in high school and enrolled in college as a math/science major.

 One day in a physics course, the professor showed her examination to an auditorium filled with science students. "Here's a young woman who wants to become a physicist and adds 2 and 2 and gets 5."

 Later she explained, "A hundred discouraging comments about my math abilities came back to me in that humiliating moment. I went down to the Records

Office and changed my major to English. In retrospect, I wonder if I did the right thing. After all, the achievement score that convinced my counselor I should avoid math was in the 96th percentile (as opposed to the 99th percentile in English). And except for that stupid arithmetic error, I got a perfect score and the highest in the class on that physics test."

In both of these cases, the subjects were labeled non-math-types—labels that ultimately affected their career choices. The first subject became a high school football coach, the second an English teacher. And their experiences are by no means atypical.

Stereotyping actually attacks from the inside as well as the outside. Externally, it affects the way teachers and classmates perceive us. Internally, it affects the way we perceive ourselves because unconsciously we often accept others' stereotypes of us. The subject in the first case study accepted in grade school that he was not a math type and behaved accordingly. The subject in the second case study struggled against the label until the incident in her college physics class.

Because stereotyping limits choices and skews perceptions, we can say that it disenfranchises. In math it works opposite to the empowering methods we discussed in the last chapter. A self-proclaimed elitist once told me, "The world is divided into two types of people—those who can do math and those who cannot. In the technological age the cannot's will serve the can's." Eradicating this type of thinking from math instruction and math learning means greater freedom for students and teachers to do their best and succeed in math studies.

Preventing Harmful Math Stereotypes

As with math anxiety, the best approach to math stereotyping is to prevent it. Prevention calls for measures that affect both the affective and the cognitive domains of learning.

1. *Teaching the curriculum:* Watering down the curriculum or inflating grades perpetuates disadvantages. To ensure that all students have equal opportunity, all must study the same things, but they need not study in the same way. While I have never found gender differences in math-learning ability, I have found some differences in math-learning styles. Generally, the girls in my classes ask more *why* questions, while the boys ask more *what* questions; the kinds of questions asked by girls often lead to more abstract kinds of explanations than those generally asked by the boys; the girls want to work out each step, while the boys want short-cuts; the girls like to wrestle with a difficult problem at home while the boys prefer to problem-solve in class; and so forth. Accommodating diversity calls for diversifying methods—for example, offering choices in testing and assignment media and allowing students to set their own pace or access the help that works best for them.

Equal opportunity also requires evaluating all students by the same standards. At the BIA school I mentioned earlier, some of the teachers graded high in order to build confidence and self-esteem. Instead, they created a false complacency—a bubble waiting to be popped.

2. *Keeping instruction integrated:* Some schools have attempted to deal with gender stereotypes by segregating math classes. Girls study in one class, boys in another. Although the girls themselves seem to like this arrangement, their comments suggest it confirms a negative stereotype:

> "I like studying without the boys. This way they can't make fun of us if we make mistakes."
> "In an all-girls class, we have a chance to ask questions."
> "The boys ruin the curve. Now we have a chance to get good grades."

Segregation by gender or by any other innate factor, either in classes or in small groups, emphasizes differences and perpetuates stereotypes. While integration does not guarantee equal opportunity, it at least creates a level playing field. The rest is up to the teacher. Giving equal question–answer time to all groups, calling on girls and boys equally, giving equal doses of praise and encouragement—all are conscious measures to combat unconscious barriers.

3. *Establishing a multicultural perspective:* A distinguishing feature of traditional math instruction is its lack of context. Like teaching history as dates rather than people and events, teaching mathematics without its human context makes it less accessible and more resistant to humanistic learning and teaching styles. It also helps promote the myth that mathematics is a white, Western subject. It is not. Moreover, the West's role in developing concepts and methods has been vastly overrated. For example, the theorem attributed to Pythagoras was demonstrated in China and India hundreds of years earlier.

Providing the historical background is a start, but learning by doing always excels over learning by being told. Children experience multicultural math when they learn to do basic calculations on an abacus; experiment with India's lattice multiplication; or discover the superiority of the Mayan calendar by comparing it to the Gregorian, Julian, Jewish, and Islamic calendars.

The estimated number of categories of identifiably different kinds or types or fields or areas of mathematics exceeds three thousand—and it is growing. To think that this number of categories would be the sole province of one cultural perspective or one type of thinking or even a handful of certified geniuses in mathematics is ludicrous. Because every people and every region of the world have made contributions to mathematics, studying the concepts can and should be inclusive rather than exclusive. Jaime Escalante boosted the confidence of his Latino students by reminding them: "Your ancestors developed these ideas. You have it in your genes." The historical context enables us to say the same thing to *all* of our students: "Your ancestors could do math; you can do math."

Freeing Teachers and Students from Harmful Math Stereotypes

Everyone is a math type. I believe this, and every student and teacher should believe it, too. If they do not, they can be convinced. Again, showing is more effective than telling, and doing is even more effective than showing. My program for helping students see themselves as math types follows six basic show-and-do steps.

1. I *show* students that I personally enjoy math by putting on my math-is-fun performance—laughing, joking, doing math tricks.
2. I *show* them that they can enjoy math by doing puzzles and playing math games with them.
3. I *show* them that they can succeed in math by assigning "success" activities—projects that combine high interest with no-wrong-answer products.
4. I gradually increase the challenge of activities and assignments while maintaining a high-interest level.
5. I ask for, expect, and receive my students' best efforts.
6. I keep working—teaching, tutoring, encouraging—and the students keep working—studying, testing, collaborating, retesting—until they succeed.

A type of immersion therapy, the program in effect forces students to live, breathe, eat, and sleep math. The result? A shift in perceptions, in attitude, in self-esteem, and in performance. If being a non–math type means failing at math, then succeeding at math means being a math type. Therefore, when an entire class succeeds (as in Jaime Escalante's calculus classes), we have an entire class of math types. In effect, the harmful, disenfranchising stereotype has been replaced with a positive, empowering self-image.

Questions for Thought and Discussion

1. Have you ever experienced or observed the effects of stereotyping generally? Of math stereotyping specifically? Discuss its impact on you and others.
2. Do you yourself entertain any stereotypes about mathematics and about those who excel or do not excel at math?
3. How do you feel about multitrack math curricula—a survival track for those who are not expected to attend college, an ac-celerated track for those expected to enter technical fields, and an appreciation track for those interested in the arts or the humanities?
4. Recall your own training in mathematics. From those experiences, what conclusions, if any, might you draw about the cultural or historical background of the subject?

Activities

1. Develop a learning module on calendars. Use calendars from various times and places. Include information about history, astronomy, and anthropology.
2. Develop a learning module on multiplication. Include examples and demonstrations of Egyptian, Mayan, Chinese, or other cultural contributions to multiplica-

tion. Have students explain the specific contributions made by various cultures.
3. Survey the media for examples of harmful math stereotypes. Explain stereotyping to your students; then present and discuss the stereotypes. Had the students already seen the examples? Was their reaction to the examples different after the discussion?

Annotated List of Readings

Davis, Philip J., and Reuben Hersh. *The Mathematical Experience.* Boston: Houghton Mifflin, 1981. *Classic treatment of what mathematics is, what it was, and what it is going to be by two eminent mathematicians.*

Feingold, A. "Cognitive Gender Differences are Disappearing." *American Psychologist 43,* no. 2 (1988): 95–103. *One of the first studies to report diminishing gender differences across cohort groups from 1947 to 1980.*

Hogben, Lancelot. *Mathematics for the Million.* New York: W. W. Norton, 1983, 1993. *Classic work on the historical development of math topics and problems.*

Makes concepts accessible and the study of math humorous and entertaining.

Marshall, Sandra P., and J. D. Smith. "Sex Differences in Learning Mathematics: A Longitudinal Study with Item and Error Analysis." *Journal of Educational Psychology 79,* no. 4 (1987): 372–381. *A readable study covering critical aspects of gender differences in the math classroom.*

Nelson, David, Joseph George Gheverghese, and Julian Williams. *Multicultural Mathematics.* New York: Oxford University Press, 1993. *Must reading. Links concepts and issues to math and culture.*

12

$$\boxed{}$$

Fearless Mathematicians

I began this book by talking about the multiple faces of math anxiety. Throughout, we have learned to recognize math anxiety in many of its disguises: the teacher who is too creative or too right-brained to teach math; the teacher who sidesteps math with computer or group activities; the student who consistently "forgets" homework, avoids tests, and daydreams during math lessons. Acknowledging the potential for math anxiety and working to prevent it; recognizing the existence of math anxiety and working to cure it—all are important adjuncts to teaching mathematics in the elementary school.

Equally important, however, are the corollaries—that is, acknowledging the potential for math confidence and working to promote it, and recognizing the existence of math confidence and working to strengthen it. Our goal, in short, is not simply to cope with math anxiety but to transcend it—to develop fearless mathematicians.

I do not mean that we are trying to turn every child into a superhero of mathematics—able to surmount the most difficult problems at a single bound. Nor do I mean that children will no longer need to struggle with math.

To be a fearless mathematician means to meet problems head on, to encounter difficulties and cope, and to struggle without panicking. In other words, fearless mathematicians are those who conceive problems as challenges, who face those challenges, and who turn stress into eustress rather than distress. In terms of problem solving, these are the troubleshooters. Fearful or math-anxious students approach problems in an either–or fashion. If they instantly recognize the problem type and know what to do, they proceed; if the problem is unfamiliar or the solution elusive, they panic. Fearless problem solvers encounter the unknown and troubleshoot. They come at it from one angle, and if that does not work, they try another and another and another until they succeed.

Creating fearless mathematicians calls for more than anxiety-free teaching and learning; it requires a mountain-climbing, over-the-top attitude and the development of a something-for-everything grab bag of working tools, strategies, and experiences. It requires basically an educational experience that matches real-life demands for mathematical skills—unpredictable, diverse, immediate, urgent, and nonnegotiable.

Several days ago I was at the checkout counter of a local supermarket. I had kept a running tally of items in my head as I shopped so that I knew that the cashier, a young man in his mid- to late teens, had shortchanged me by 86 cents. When I called the matter to his attention, he at first cited the authority of the cash register slip, then tried to give me two dollars instead of 86 cents. It took an assistant manager and a hand-held calculator to straighten out the numbers mess and give me the correct change.

This is not numbers dysfunction at its worst, but it is typical. Not the least disturbing aspect of the incident was the cashier's anxiety—fear at my first question, panic and inability to think when I persisted. As I left the store, I heard him muttering, "I always hated math."

What would it have taken to turn that cashier into a fearless mathematician?

1. *A challenging curriculum:* Easy requirements and simple exercises do not produce fearless problem solvers, nor does the lack of discipline. "No pain, no gain" is no longer an acceptable slogan for physical education, but a related slogan, "no stress, no progress," still works for learning math. The educational system that produced my cashier emphasizes the feel-good philosophy of education. If you like it, do it; if you don't like it, forget it. He may have passed all of his math courses; he may even have passed the quantitative part of the system's high school basic-skills test. But he could not handle a simple math challenge—the need to respond quickly and effectively to questions about numbers and basic operations like adding and subtracting.

2. *Eustressful learning experiences:* A stressless learning environment, as we have seen, may produce some benefits affectively but few cognitively. Meaningful learning calls for those mountain-climbing experiences. I do not, of course, mean putting students on the spot, running them through their paces, sharing through scaring, or any of the other toughening-up techniques dear to the hearts of Marine Corps drill instructors. I do mean creating situations in and outside the classroom that stretch abilities to the limit without exceeding or violating these limits.

3. *Balanced affective and cognitive development:* I am sure my cashier could add and subtract. Given a quiet room and pencil and paper, he could undoubtedly have come up with an accurate total for my rather long shopping list; probably, he even could have found the error that resulted in the incorrect total and change. But he panicked—the distressed state that frequently overrides even simple cognitive

processes. What robbed the cashier of his ability to add and subtract was not the cognitive nature of the problem itself but the affective context of the problem—a supermarket line where people were waiting and a supervisor was watching. This suggests to me that the young man had been taught what I call isolated math—one place, one time, one way to solve problems and a few well-defined problem-solving contexts. Outside well-defined parameters, he was literally helpless.

For education in the affective domain to keep pace with education in the cognitive domain, students must experience affective diversity—that is, learning in diverse contexts, under diverse conditions, for diverse purposes. In the case of the cashier, training for his job should have included thinking-on-his-feet math; but his schooling also shortchanged him by neglecting the affective side of his math learning.

4. *Respect for accuracy and detail:* It is difficult to have confidence in approximations: we never feel on totally solid ground when our calculations are "about," "around," "rounded off," "close enough," "working figures," or "guesstimates." Yet our world approximates constantly. Our calculators round off final decimal places; even the IRS requires us to round off cents to dollars. Respect for accuracy—for giving exact change, for paying debts "to the penny," for charging what is right "and not a penny more"—is being lost, and with it confidence in even the simplest calculations.

Consider the Pentium chip debacle. The key component of thousands of PCs makes errors in division—small errors, admittedly, but errors nonetheless. What disturbs me most about the incident is not the errors themselves but the initial lack of concern by both the company and the industry. The errors, we were told, were minor, inconsequential, within an acceptable margin.

The margin-for-error concept is actually hostile to the development of some basic math skills. (Even after years as a statistician, I have never adopted the mentality of accepting one type of error over another.) Paying meticulous attention to accuracy—computing to the last decimal point, recording remainders, carrying out instead of rounding off—develops a confidence in calculations inaccessible to the overestimators and approximators. The difference between saying "My calculations are correct" and "My figures are in the ballpark" is the difference between mastery and acquaintance.

5. *Development of "math sense":* Having math sense means having a sense for a right fit: for feeling when answers are right or wrong, for knowing that something is amiss in either process or product prior to identifying the exact error, for intuiting correctness.

Several years ago I received a light bill that quintupled my usual monthly charge. When I called the utility company, I spoke to several people before I finally encountered a troubleshooter. She looked at the computer records of my bill and my average monthly usage and spotted the problem instantly: the meter reader had added an extra zero to his figures.

Math sense is not developed overnight, nor is it produced by math programs that require students to study concepts but leave the tedious business of calculations to computers or calculators. Supposedly, focusing on concept development while excluding the menial tasks of calculating strengthens students cognitively and prepares them for more abstract thought. However, if a concept cannot be applied to even a simple problem, does the student really know the concept? What if students needed an entire complex of concepts for a more challenging problem? If they are not able to apply even a single concept, how can they deal with a challenge of greater complexity? At many levels and in many math categories, conceptualization without calculation, though certainly abstract, is also meaningless, whereas calculation without conceptualization is learning by rote. In other words, calculation and conceptualization need each other: they interact in ways necessary for mutual benefits. Although top-down thinking may sound conceptually appealing to some math educators, it is actually bottom-up thinking that builds strong conceptual frameworks that eventually enable one to conceptualize from the top down. When students are first introduced to a concept—and in elementary level mathematics, every concept is new—bottom-up thinking is necessary. Before they are ready for top-down thinking at the most abstract levels, students must first build a strong theoretical and computational background so that top-down thinking is appropriate, productive, and natural.

The math sense demonstrated by the utility company troubleshooter emerges only from hands-on experience across a wide variety of problems at different levels of complexity. In the case of my math-anxious cashier, math sense would develop even now if he would practice running totals in his head while he checks customers out and not rely—without thought—on the accuracy of his cash register. There were actually two math errors that he did not sense in my bill—the error in the total dollar amount and an error in the total number of items. The register had counted one 41 cent item three times, so that I was triple charged plus triple taxed for it.

6. *Development of math tenacity:* Teaching students to keep working until they succeed could be the cornerstone to building a fearless mathematics program. Play-until-you-win is a foreign concept in education—a field typically ruled by bells or buzzers, drop-dead deadlines, and timed tests. But quitting before you solve a problem breeds frustrated rather than fearless mathematicians. Unsolved problems leave gaps in understanding, and those gaps create anxiety.

Probably the most fearless mathematician in any of my classes was D.C. Neither a prodigy nor a math whiz, D.C. was described by previous teachers as "mathematically challenged." His highest grade in math had been a low C, a gift from a teacher who wanted to encourage him. But D.C. liked math, and he was determined to succeed. During the first class D.C. took with me, he studied hard, came to my tutoring hours, and earned a solid C. I was satisfied, but D.C. was not. "I can do better," he told me before summer vacation. Then, for that entire summer, D.C.

thought about math. He reworked every problem from our course until he understood them backwards and forwards. I had noticed that he kept making the same kinds of mistakes over and over again; he practiced until he not only did not make those mistakes but also could recognize the traps before he fell into them. The next fall he was back, but in my advanced algebra course. He told me, "Don't worry, Dr. Martinez, I can do this. I have been thinking about math all summer, and I understand it now." And he did! From that point on, he scored high on tests and received A's in every math course afterwards. He became a math major, completing two degrees in mathematics—and the last I heard about D.C. was that he was working on his doctorate in applied mathematics.

D.C. was a tenacious worker who would not accept lack of understanding or lack of success. He did not demand instant success, but he did demand success. Why do I call him a fearless mathematician? Because he did not let fear or failure stop or divert him from studying math. He continued to study math when all external indicators suggested that he stop: when his grades and even his teachers said he could not do math and when his own mind told him he did not understand many math concepts.

For many teachers, encouraging students to become fearless mathematicians starts with becoming fearless mathematicians themselves. I do not mean that every elementary teacher should take advanced math courses or earn advanced degrees in mathematics. Rather, teachers must be fearless about the mathematics they know and teach in elementary school—to know and understand every concept so well that they can field questions and problem-solve on their feet, sense errors in mathematical thinking as well as errors in numbers computations, and demonstrate positive affective as well as cognitively based problem-solving strategies. Positive math affect remains fundamental to positive math teaching. It means demonstrating determination and anticipation rather than frustration and anxiety when struggling with unknowns; showing persistence and patience in negotiating tedious steps; and experiencing the surge of elation that comes with an insight or a difficulty surmounted. Just as math-anxious teachers produce math-anxious students, teachers who approach math fearlessly produce students who approach math fearlessly.

Developing Fearless Problem-Solving Strategies

Being a fearless mathematician is not so much a set condition or quality as an ongoing process, and the process calls on resources from both the cognitive and affective domains of learning. Like anxiety, fearlessness and confidence emerge from our math histories. Learning experiences, attitudes about learning, knowledge structures, associations, beliefs, assumptions—all provide a context for math study that points toward confidence, anxiety, or something in between. Throughout this book, I have proposed teaching and learning strategies as well as materials and activities that work against developing math anxiety and for developing math confidence. Taken together, the elements of positive math teaching and learning comprise a repertoire of effective problem-solving strategies that will help both students and teachers become fearless mathematicians.

Problem-Solving Strategies:

1. *Turning distress into eustress:* Stress becomes a problem when it triggers distress, the negative response that handicaps learning. To exchange distress for eustress calls, first, for redefining the conditions of the problem—instead of a threat, we have a challenge—and, second, for reversing the response to the problem—instead of "flight," we have "fight."

2. *Rewriting math histories:* A negative math history is not written in concrete; it can be edited and rewritten by substituting good experiences for bad and successes for failures.

3. *Verbalizing:* Using the familiar to understand the unfamiliar can start with translating math language into ordinary language. Writing out or talking out a problem activates the complex cognitive processes associated with language; it also helps focus and organize inquiry and reveal insights.

4. *Engaging the problem:* Dealing with a problem by avoiding it is an example of a failed problem-solving strategy. Making a conscious decision to face and work through a problem (whether cognitive or affective) works like your computer's power switch: none of the programs can run until you turn on the power.

5. *Accepting unknowns:* Inflexible teaching models foster inflexible performances. When there is no tolerance for the unknown—for problems posed in new ways, for unfamiliar concepts, contexts, and approaches—math work becomes mass production, repetition of procedures and results that are already known. In true problem solving, unknowns signal *go* rather than *stop.*

6. *Playing through:* Exchanging math work for math play has two special advantages as a problem-solving strategy. First it changes the problem-solving context from threatening to nonthreatening. Second, it alters the problem solver's perspective, providing a new frame of reference and a fresh look at the problem.

7. *Rehearsing:* Unthinking repetition becomes a conditioned response—habitual rather than thoughtful action. Rehearsing, however, means walking through a problem again and again but each time looking for something new or different.

8. *Collaborating:* Working together to solve problems forces us to articulate what we know and what we do not know about the problem and to weigh alternatives for the best approach or data or solution.

9. *Working backwards:* Giving students access to answer books and solutions manuals alters a major condition of classroom problem solving. Instead of looking for specific answers, they are looking for ways to find answers. Therefore, when working from beginning to end fails, students can try working from

end to beginning. Reversing steps engages different and to some extent more complex cognitive skills. Affectively, it changes a clueless mystery into a jigsaw puzzle. Students may not have a complete picture, but they at least know the outline of the missing parts.

10. *Rewriting the problem:* Trekkies will remember this strategy as Captain Kirk's way of beating Starfleet's *Kobayashi Maru* test: he rewrote a no-win command problem to allow himself to win. Sometimes rewriting and changing very difficult math problems can place problem solvers closer to solving the original problem by putting them in control and also by allowing them to demonstrate what they do know.

11. *Rejecting stereotypes and limitations:* Most affective blocks to math problem solving begin with "I can't because. . . ." I can't do math because I'm a girl or a minority or because my parents can't do math or my teacher couldn't teach math. Replacing the "I can't's" with "I can's" calls for developing a new set of experiences and assumptions: "I can do math because I'm smart, because I'm a descendant of the Mayans and I carry math intelligence in my genes, because I study hard and get good grades, because I want to do math."

12. *Guessing and testing:* George Polya (whose classic *Mathematical Discovery* is listed in the annotated readings at the end of this chapter) applies the scientific method to mathematical problem solving in three words: "guess and test" (pp. 156–157). Guessing solutions and testing their effectiveness means both working through problems again and again and approaching those problems from every possible direction.

Strategies like these promote fearless problem solving when they are vigorously applied and aggressively stockpiled. Like working capital, problem-solving strategies that are "owned" through mastery and made active through constant use multiply our resources and increase our security. The more ways we know to solve a problem, the more confident we will be about solving it. In addition, the more strategies we have at our disposal, the longer we will keep working on the problem; the longer we work, the greater the opportunities for solving it.

I once taught math at a small school that used pre- and posttesting throughout the math program. One of my colleagues decided that the best way to ensure a high success rate on the posttest was to teach for the test. He identified the specific types of problems that appeared on the posttest and taught and drilled his students in one method of solving each type of problem. His one-method/one-solution math teaching accomplished its goal. His students performed adequately on the posttest, and they learned to apply a limited number of procedures to a limited number of problems. But they could not "think math." Given the same problems in a different dress, such as words instead of numbers, they could not function. "We don't know what you want," they would say, or "We haven't had this yet." In other words, what they had learned was the trained-bear version of doing math—small sequences of actions and procedures that mimicked math thought but had little real meaning for

FIGURE 12-1   **Fearful/Fearless Mathematics Chart**

Characteristics of Fearful Mathematics Learning	Characteristics of Fearless Mathematics Learning
Learning by rote	Learning by concept
Restricted applications	Unrestricted applications
Inflexible conditions	Flexible conditions
Lock-step process	Reversible, revisable process
Monomethod problem solving	Multimethod problem solving
Emphasis on drill	Emphasis on problem solving
One-chance testing	Many-chances testing
Negative motivation	Positive motivation
Low expectations	High expectations
Acceptance of stereotypes	Rejection of stereotypes
All-or-nothing thinking	Something-is-better-than-nothing thinking
Minimal exposure	Maximum involvement
Teacher ownership of information	Shared ownership of information
Proscribed goals	Negotiated goals
Learning in a vacuum	Learning in context
Imitation	Creativity
Passive learning	Active learning

them. Challenged to justify his methods, my colleague responded, "They don't really need to *know* this stuff; they just have to *look like they know* it."

Cognitively, the difference between knowing something and appearing to know it is the difference between action and passivity: the mind is turned on in the former, off in the latter. Affectively, the person who can "think math" has every reason to approach math problems without fear and with confidence of success, while the person who only appears to know has every reason to fear failure. Figure 12-1 above highlights characteristics of fearful and fearless mathematics learning.

Although my one-method/one-solution colleague considered himself to be a liberal, student-oriented teacher, he taught what I call icebox math—processed, packaged, and frozen in place. Pedagogically, the approach is simple and straightforward, with well-defined goals and easily measured outcomes. But true learning tends to be messy. It draws from and spills over into real life in ways that defy the neat outlines of lessons plans and the simple closure of pre- and posttested study.

Scenario #1: One-Method/One-Solution Math Lesson

Objective: To figure percentages

Method: Multiplication with decimal equivalents

Special Concerns: Manipulation of decimal points

Teacher: Sometimes we need to figure a percentage of another number. The best way to do this is to change the percent to a decimal and multiply.

So if we start with the number 100 and we want to take 25% of that, we have to first change 25% to a decimal. We do that by moving the decimal two places to the left to give us .25.

Then we can set up and work the problem like this:

$$
\begin{array}{r}
100 \\
\times\ .25 \\
\hline
500 \\
200 \\
\hline
25.00
\end{array}
$$

Student #1: Couldn't we also divide 100 by 4?

Student #2: Or just move the decimal over two places to match the zeroes in 100?

Teacher: No, I said we would learn the best way to take percentages and multiplying is the best way. Forget other ways. They'll just confuse you.

Scenario #2: Many-Methods/Many-Solutions Math Lesson

Objective: To figure percentages

Teacher: Can you think of any situation in which you might need to figure a percentage of something?

Student #1: When you want to know how much interest you're paying on your credit cards.

Student #2: When you need to figure a 15% tip for dinner.

Teacher: Okay, let's say you are paying 15% interest or a 15% tip on $100. How would you find the amount?

Student #2: My dad always says to figure out a tip take 10%, then add half of that.

Teacher: How much is 10% of $100?

Student #2: $10.

Teacher: And half of that?

Student #2: $5, so the tip would be $15.

Teacher: Could you use the same method if you wanted to leave a 20% tip.

Student #3: Sure. Just take 10% and multiply by 2 for $20.

Student #4: Or divide by 5.

Teacher: Why divide by 5?

Student #4: Twenty percent of something is the same thing as 1/5 of it.

Teacher: What if we start with a number like $189? You have just charged the latest Nintendo game to your mom's credit card, and she has said you will pay the whole amount with interest, even if it takes a year. If the interest rate is 16%

per year (and you have too many other debts to start paying before next year), how much could this cost you in interest alone?

Student #2: At least $28 or $29.

Teacher: How did you get that figure?

Student #2: Sixteen percent is close to 15%, so I used the same way as before.

Teacher: Is there another method that would give us a more exact answer?

Student #1: We could change 16% to a decimal and multiply by that.

Teacher: Why would that work?

Student #1: It works with the first problem: 15% is .15, and multiplying by $100 gets us $15.

The lesson in Scenario #1 ends with a stop sign. The students have been shown one way to figure percentages and been discouraged from experimenting with other methods. The lesson in Scenario #2 is open ended, with students encouraged to guess and test or inquire and explain their way through as many methods as possible. After a regime of similar learning experiences, students in the first class will expect math recipes—tested and tried formulas for processing data and producing cookbook solutions. Asked to guesstimate answers or find alternative paths to solutions, they would probably react with confusion, possibly followed by resentment and even fear. Students in the second class, accustomed to experimenting with numbers and exploring concepts, would be more likely to respond fearlessly to the same problems and to feel challenged rather than intimidated by them.

Becoming a fearless mathematician or a fearless teacher of mathematics will probably not happen overnight. You will know that you are becoming fearless when teaching or studying math is no longer an externally driven task but internally motivated and emotionally as well as intellectually satisfying. You will know that your students are becoming fearless mathematicians when they enjoy math, look forward to math courses, work persistently on the most difficult problems, and attack the subject with all systems on "go"—asking questions, making comments, trying and making mistakes, then trying and finding answers. Not every student or every teacher can or should become a math professional, but all of us can and should master the skills and concepts that impact our daily lives and experience the confidence and freedom from anxiety that come from knowing and doing math well.

Questions for Thought and Discussion

1. What problem-solving strategies do you use in doing math problems?
2. What additional problem-solving strategies can you add to those listed in this chapter?
3. Do you believe that everyone can become a fearless mathematician? Why or why not?
4. What changes (if any) would you make in your school's math curriculum to promote fearless mathematics?

Activities

1. Write a module for a math curriculum that places concepts in real-life contexts.
2. Write a scenario for an open-ended multiple-methods lesson on a basic concept or procedure. Include dialogue and computations.
3. Write your own math autobiography. Include a math history—what happened in past math learning and teaching and the effect of those experiences on you—and a math future—what you plan to do to rewrite and change negative elements in your math history and to strengthen and extend positive elements.

Annotated List of Readings

Bransford, John D., and Barry S. Stein. *The Ideal Problem Solver: A Guide for Improving Thinking, Learning, and Creativity.* 2nd ed. New York: W. H. Freeman, 1993. *A systematic approach to problem solving. Uses IDEAL as an acronym for strategies that address different stages in the problem-solving process.*

Polya, George. *Mathematical Discovery: On Understanding, Learning, and Teaching Problem Solving.* New York: Wiley, 1981. *Combined edition of original two-volume work. Presents case histories of solutions and advice for teachers in the context of practical problem-solving strategies.*

Appendix: Math Behavior Self-Change Project

Math behavior can be changed and so can negative thought patterns. Yet many math-anxious people feel as if they are victims of fate. The project represents an opportunity to observe carefully and attempt systematically to change math-anxious behaviors or thought patterns. Your self-change project will involve five sections, to be presented in a written paper or journal.

1. *The behavior or thought pattern:* In this section you should carefully describe the specific math-anxious behavior or thought pattern you choose to change and also describe how you decide to measure it.

a. First, choose a math-anxious behavior that you want to change and that you can change. This may be more difficult than it sounds at first. It must be a behavior or thought pattern that is specific enough that you can count it or measure it in some other quantitative way. In other words, it is not sufficient to say that you want to increase your math confidence. Your terms must be operationally defined (for example, you might count the number of times you feel worry or doubt while doing math problems or the number of positive statements you make about math while doing math problems and so forth). Remember that while behaviors are observable and generally measurable, thought patterns are unobservable but measurable. As long as you can measure it reliably, it qualifies as being operationally defined. Include a brief history of your struggles and your ideas about the causes of this behavior.

b. Describe the unit of analysis. You must decide what the unit of measurement will be. Some possibilities are times per day you study math; minutes per day you study math; number of math problems you work per day; numbers of positive and negative statements you make about math per day; ratings of how strong a feeling is, or how distressing on a 1–10 scale some math anxiety is.

2. *Baseline/record keeping:* In writing this section of your self-change project describe the baseline and how you kept records.

a. *Baseline:* Keep records for seven to ten days of the math-anxious-related behavior or thought pattern you want to change as it spontaneously occurs. In this stage of your project do not attempt to alter or modify naturally occurring behavior. This will give you a baseline with which to compare changes (gains, losses, etc.) over several weeks.

b. Decide how to keep track of behavior you are observing. In general, it is better to keep records throughout the day than to write them down at the end of the day; our memories can become selective.

3. *Intervention procedure (three-week minimum)*

a. Decide on and describe your goals and subgoals. Your final goal could be completing a specific number of units in a self-paced math course; increasing positive comments or decreasing negative comments by a specific number; or attending a number of tutorial sessions per week that you had previously avoided. Your subgoals should be realistic daily or weekly accomplishments that increase your chances of reaching the final goal.

b. Choose reinforcement(s) that will optimize your chances of success. Systematically reward yourself as you systematically change your behavior or thought pattern.

c. You may opt to develop an alternative behavior or thought pattern which makes the frequency of performing or thinking along certain lines improbable. For example, if you replace negative statements with positive ones or negative thoughts with positive ones, your alternative can be the focus of your intervention.

4. *Results:* In this section of your project, describe the results.
a. Graph the results:

    Baseline results
    Intervention results

b. Describe the results:
    Example:
    a) During baseline the number of positive statements about math averaged .7 times per day while the number of negative statements about math averaged 28 times per day.

b) By the end of the third week of intervention the mean number of negative statements decreased to 7 times per day, while the mean number of positive statements increased to 18 times per day.

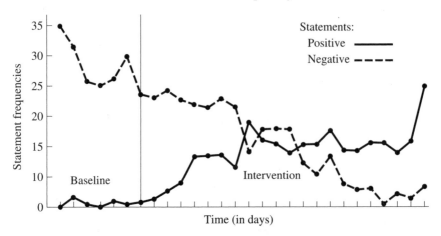

5. *Discussion:* In this section discuss the effectiveness or the lack of it concerning the procedure used and the difficulties encountered.

a. Did you learn anything about what factors are important in controlling behavior?

b. How successful was your attempt to change the behavior or thought pattern?

c. Did it change in the direction you had hoped? Why or why not?

d. If you were successful in making a change, how likely do you think it is that the change will last over the months ahead?

Index